FIRST DO NO HARM

PROGRESSIVE EDUCATION IN A TIME OF EXIS-TENTIAL RISK

FIRST DO NO HARM

PROGRESSIVE EDUCATION IN A TIME OF EXISTENTIAL RISK

STEVE NELSON

GARN PRESS
NEW YORK, NY

Published by Garn Press, LLC
New York, NY
www.garnpress.com

Book and cover design by Benjamin J. Taylor/Garn Press
Cover image by Steve Nelson

First Edition, November 2016

Library of Congress Control Number: 2016954494

Publisher's Cataloging-in-Publication Data

Names: Nelson, Steve
Title: First do no harm : progressive education in a time of existential risk / Steve
    Nelson.
Description: First edition. | New York : Garn Press, 2016. | Includes bibliographical
references.
Identifiers: LCCN 2016954494 | ISBN 978-1-942146-47-6 (pbk.) | ISBN 978-1-942146-
    48-3 (hardcover) | ISBN 978-1-942146-49-0 (Kindle ebook)
Subjects: LCSH: Progressive education. | Educational change. | Educational
    equalization. | Democracy and education. | Charter schools. | Human beings-
    -Effect of climate on. | BISAC: EDUCATION / Educational Policy & Reform /
    General. | EDUCATION / Philosophy, Theory & Social Aspects. | EDUCATION
    / Education Policy & Reform / Charter Schools. | EDUCATION / History. |
    EDUCATION / Comparative.
Classification: LCC LB1027.3 .N45 2016 (print) | LCC LB1027.3 (ebook) | DDC 371.3-
    -dc23.

Contents

Introduction by

Matt Damon

Things have gone very wrong in education in recent years. Many of us know this, but few of us really understand what has happened and why. But Steve Nelson does. And in this book, he helps us understand education in a way that deepens our awareness of the profound impact education has on children's lives and the society and world we live in.

I guess it's not unusual to know someone personally, as I do Steve, yet be awed by what they do. Steve has written a book that is really exceptional. And it comes at a critical time when our education system is faltering and our planet is plagued with what he calls existential threats. As the book unfolds, we see more and more how and why progressive education is an essential part of solving the problems of unprecedented magnitude that we face.

In progressive education, as Steve tells us, there is respect for children, how they develop, how they are internally motivated, how they learn best when they have some voice in the learning process. The visual and performing arts and music are a critical part of progressive education, not frills. I know this in my blood and bones. I wouldn't be who I am or where I am today if I hadn't gone to the progressive public elementary, middle and high schools I attended. Teachers in those schools respected me and my interest in theater, they trusted me to think for myself, to make choices about my own learning. The whole school community mattered – I learned how to collaborate with others, to solve problems with them. Progressive educators intentionally design their programs to lead students toward becoming adults who will be engaged citizens committed to economic and social justice.

I am concerned about our planet and the existential threats Steve identifies – climate change, nuclear threat, terrorism, social and economic injustice. I am concerned about the growing divide in our society and the increasing intolerance we are witnessing. In progressive education, students learn to respect different cultures, races, points of view. They experience being part of a democratic community where all voices are equal, all have responsibility, and where compassion for others is encouraged.

The assumptions that drive most education policy and practices today are mistaken. They shortchange kids and cause harm. We have schools driven by data and testing, there is less music, arts, play, social interaction and child choice. Steve rebuts the flawed assumptions of the uniform factory approach to education. But he goes even further. As pages unfold, we see more and more that we need the progressive education revolution he is calling for.

This is ultimately a hopeful book. Steve spells out a vision of real education reform that we just might be ready for now. His Bill of Educational Rights, based on the best of what is known from science and theory about human development and children's learning, should be our manifesto. All children deserve a progressive education, not just the privileged few. All children deserve an education that will enliven their lives with joy and possibility and help them contribute to the betterment of society and our planet.

Matt Damon

Los Angeles, July 27th, 2016

Preface

I am mindful of the position from which I write. Those of us in independent schools enjoy great privilege. This privilege allows us to draw our students into deeply satisfying and thoughtful lives. But we must recognize that these experiences should not be limited to only those children who are wealthy and/or lucky enough to enroll in our schools. Non-sectarian private schools enroll only about 6% of America's children.

So what about the other millions of children? Do we who carry privilege also bear responsibility? I think so.

Most independent schools see service learning or community service as parts of their mission. But too often service to the community is a form of noblesse oblige. We must remind ourselves that charity is a sad necessity that fills the holes that injustice leaves behind. We must insist that our students understand the difference between charity and justice.

Our private school privilege carries a companion responsibility. We must take positions on public policy. We can partner with public schools and defend teachers. We can lobby for public school funding and fight for educational equity. We can speak out against rigid, humiliating disciplinary practices. We can advocate for the arts in all schools. We can make our programs and resources available to less privileged schools in our communities. We can write books.

Acknowledgments are necessary. I must begin with my immediate family members, who have encouraged, inspired and insisted on whatever decent qualities I bring to my work. My wife Wendy has made me a better person and I love her for that and lots else. My daughter Jennifer and son Christopher and his partner Megan are not only loved, but I am proud beyond expression of the good work they do in their own lives. My granddaughter Quinn keeps me on my toes and used to be my best friend, until she grew up and our fantastic rocket sled rides became just a fond memory. I'm getting over it – slowly. And my other grandchildren, Maddie and Jack, keep me younger and happier than I would otherwise be.

I must thank all the great educators who have been part of my life at the Calhoun School. My understanding of progressive education has come from their work, not out of my imagination. I'm deeply appreciative of Calhoun's Trustees, who have trusted me with their school and allowed a sabbatical, during which time I wrote most of this book.

Finally, I'm grateful to Denny Taylor and the Garn Press family – not just for publishing the book. The mission of Garn Press is admirable, courageous and desperately needed in a time of existential risk. I am mighty proud to be associated with the inspirational work they do.

Introduction

Progressive Education and Existential Risk

The Existential Risk

We kneeled beneath our desks, terrified – and skeptical. It was the 1950's and my classmates and I were among the many American children being trained to "duck and cover." The idea of an atomic bomb attack was acutely terrifying. I'd seen images of Hiroshima, even at age seven. But even at age seven, I knew my small plywood desk would be of no use against such power.

Now, 62 years later, I note that we don't subject seven year-olds to such futile exercises in regard to the nuclear threat. We just don't talk to children about these things at all. Perhaps that's for the best. Seven year-old children should not live in mortal fear because of our moral failures.

The moment my daughter was born I rediscovered terror. Holding her, pink and damp, moments after birth, I felt a sense of panic and responsibility. Partially fueled by a dollop of male grandiosity, I wondered how this fragile infant would survive in my care. The terror turned out to be fleeting and unnecessary. With or without me, she would walk, talk and make her way fiercely through the world, as would my son who was born almost exactly three years later.

And so it went. My children are grown and thriving and for several decades I've been too busy to be terrified.

But now, approaching the other bookend of my shelf life, I'm terrified again. I'm not afraid of my own death (or eagerly anticipating it). It's a lovely thing about human existence, at least for those fortunate enough to live a full arc. As the end approaches, a sense of gentle resignation seems to emerge. I don't know anyone in the "later" years who is afraid of dying.

I'm not afraid, but I'm sometimes terrified. This terror arises unbidden when I think about my three grandchildren. I imagine them in the path of nuclear incineration. I worry that they might have to navigate a barren world, facing horrible, human-induced climate events or the day when clean water becomes a precious commodity, even in our wealthy nation. I see them helpless in the face of man's inhumanity to man – genocide, bigotry, cruelty, and indifference. It is the only thing I fear about death – being gone and unable to hold them, love them if the Earth becomes inhospitable and life becomes unbearable. The thought of my grandchildren – all the world's children – suffering after I'm gone is my only hell.

It is not hyperbole to declare that we are living in a time of grave existential threat. The nuclear threat of 1950's is mere child's play compared to the world today. Russia, the UK, France, China, North Korea, India, Pakistan, and Israel all have nuclear weapons. Barack Obama has declared a 30-year $1 trillion plan to modernize our deadly nuclear arsenal.

The acceleration of climate change, as evidenced by rising global temperatures, the loss of the ice shelf and other alarming signs, should terrorize every rational person. We are losing species and biodiversity at an increasing rate and depleting Earth's resources.

Racism, religious fanaticism, and intolerance are igniting flash fires of terror all around the world, whether in the Middle East, sub-Saharan Africa, a café in Paris, a church in Charleston or a nightclub in Orlando.

The terror is not only these global threats. My childhood's "duck and cover" is today's "shelter in place," as we jeopardize our domestic tranquility by cowering before the NRA and capitulating to the irrational notion that an armed world is a safer world. So instead of fearing the Soviets, we fear ourselves. As Pogo said, "We have met the enemy and it is us."

In his last years, my good Vermont friend the late Rev. William Sloane Coffin, Jr. described himself as a "man in a hurry." His commitment to peace and justice didn't wane as his life energy ebbed. We grandparents, one and all, need to be women and men in a hurry.

Another Vermont acquaintance, the late poet grandmother Grace Paley, wrote in her poem "Responsibility" [1]:

There is no freedom without fear and bravery there is no freedom unless / earth and air and water continue and children / also continue

*It is the responsibility of the poet to be a woman to keep
an eye on this world and cry out like Cassandra, but be
/ listened to this time.*

I'm not a woman, a poet or Cassandra. I'm an educator. The response to existential risk must come on all fronts, but particularly from grandparents who are "in a hurry." This book is my modest contribution.

A progressive revolution in education must lead this response. For more than a century, education for most American children has been dull and uninspiring. Today, even in the face of these existential threats, we speak of education as if it is only vocational training. We act as though children have value only for some future economic use. Schools suppress skepticism, punish humor and silence children's imagination. Technology distracts them and distorts their sense of the world.

Our future depends on preparing today's young women and men to be thoughtful, creative, engaged citizens. They must be fully alive, in love with the natural world and each other. They must be skeptical, not compliant. They must be deeply idealistic and speak truth to power. They must see the planet as their home, not as an endless source of material goods. They must see all people as their neighbors, not as their competitors in a global contest for military and economic superiority.

Jean-Paul Sartre believed anguish to be the emotion people feel once they realize that they are responsible not just for themselves, but for all humanity.

We must feel the anguish.

Progressive Education

The phrase "progressive education" is familiar to almost anyone with a passing interest in education. Educators who embrace its tenets in schools around the world proudly use the phrase. Politicians, policy-makers and pundits frequently invoke "progressive" as shorthand for everything that is wrong with education. Since this book's title includes the phrase, it may be helpful to state clearly what I mean by it. This brief definition will be more thoroughly explicated throughout the book.

The essential idea of progressive education may be captured in two intersecting categories:

1. The democratic nature of a school community and the broad social intentions of a progressive school.

2. The historical, theoretical, philosophical, psychological and neurobiological pillars, which provide a solid foundation for progressive education practices.

While the distinctions between progressive education and conventional education are not always stark, it is reasonable to differentiate between "education and training," between "learning and being taught", and between "discovery and instruction." Conventional schools tend toward training and instruction, while progressive schools insist on learning and discovery.

Perhaps the most powerful and misunderstood facet of progressive education is the notion of democracy. Progressive schools see themselves and their students as inextricably connected to the society in which they operate. The problems and fascinations of the world around them are the problems and fascinations they examine. By contrast, in the schools of my childhood and most schools today, knowledge is in a formal literary canon and textbooks. Democracy is a vague concept or litany of historical facts to be instructed in a civics or social studies class. In a progressive school, democracy is an idea to be lived and practiced.

In a conventional school, students are seen as vessels into which authoritative adults pour "content." In a progressive school, students are seen as unique individuals, partners in learning, with their own important ideas, values and experiences. While there are many shades of grey, conventional schools tend to value and insist on compliance and conformity, while progressive schools encourage skepticism and originality. This may seem an extreme or unfair distinction, but an objective look at current educational policy and practice makes the case unambiguously. Compliance and conformity are the standard cognitive and behavioral expectations in most conventional schools.

Apart from the intentions of a school, many conventional notions of education are misguided. Three basic assumptions drive most education policy and practice and they are simply wrong:

1. All children develop at the same rate and should be able to do the same things at the same time.

2. Extrinsic structures – grades, tests, rewards, and punishments – are the most effective motivational milieu.

3. Intelligence is primarily a measure of an individual's mathematical and linguistic abilities, as measured on any number of standardized assessments, from classroom quizzes and grade level tests to college and

graduate school admissions.

Conventional schools and institutions are explicitly and/or implicitly structured around these mistaken notions. Basing education on these assumptions impedes learning for untold millions of children.

Chapters 4, 5 and 6 make a detailed case for three very different assumptions, on which progressive education is based. The psychological and neurobiological bases of progressive education emerge from several centuries of evolving knowledge about learning and human development.

1. Children develop at highly varied rates and cannot be expected to do the same things in the same way at the same time.

2. Intrinsic motivation is more durable and powerful than extrinsic motivation.

3. Human intelligence is rich and complex, and cannot be accurately valued or assessed within the rigid binary of mathematical/linguistic ability.

I devote many pages to a critique of contemporary beliefs about learning and to an unapologetic criticism of current education policy and education reform. I deeply believe that these educational practices are not only shortchanging children, they are too often harming children.

The ways we assess schools and the ways we assess children are also based almost entirely on flawed assumptions. I've spent years debating, commenting, blogging and otherwise beating my head against stubborn conventional wisdom. Making a case for progressive education cannot be done without deconstructing these assumptions, on which so many policies, practices and opinions are based.

The political and economic aspects of so-called education reform are the most visible battleground in American education. Rebutting the propaganda fomented by reformers is a necessary theme in these pages. Many others have also done – are doing – this work with incisive intelligence. Rejecting corporate education reform in this way is necessary, but insufficient.

My added contribution to this education debate is to suggest that most anti-reform advocates don't go far enough. There is widespread agreement among educators that corporate reform drives bad policy and that the standards and accountability movement went too far. But most of these folks still hold rather conventional views of learning and education practice. They believe testing is necessary – just not so much. They believe that the conventional ways of assessing children and the conventional structures of schools are basically sound. They talk about "instruction," "content," and "curriculum" as though they are the essential components of good education. I respectfully disagree.

Even the more encouraging contemporary ideas that have been highly touted in the popular media fall short. EQ (emotional quotient) or EI (emotional intelligence), for example, has gotten lots of good press. But its proponents seldom talk about fundamental change in schools. Ironically, they don't seem to recognize that conventional school structures and practices devalue the very qualities they promote.

Grit and perseverance have also become familiar buzzwords, yet the dreary school environments that require grit to survive are seldom criticized. Paul Tough, whose books have sold in the millions, provided inspiration for the Knowledge is Power Program (KIPP) Schools, whose disciplinary practices are, in a word, horrific. Many observers cite test score scandals, critique "teaching to the test", and question the reliability of test scores reported by charter schools. But even these well-meaning critics only question the credibility of the standardized test results, they don't argue that test scores are the wrong objective.

Here are a few generally accepted ideas about education that I hope to convincingly rebut:

1. Early academic work leads to future academic success.

2. High IQ or high scores on standardized tests, SAT's or ACT's are a reliable indicator of intelligence or potential.

3. You can judge the quality of a school by the measurable achievement of its students.

4. Grades and competition are important motivators and result in higher achievement.

5. Poor children, particularly children of color, need strict discipline in order to succeed.

6. Technology is a great advance in education and we should focus on producing "21st century" learners.

7. We must improve education so that our children will be competitive in the global economy.

8. Progressive education is a failed liberal experiment and has inhibited educational progress.

9. We are falling behind the rest of the world. America's schools have gotten steadily worse and corporate-led

education reform is absolutely necessary, even if it is painful.

10. Private enterprise and free markets are more efficient and effective than government, including in education.

11. "School choice" will motivate improvements in education and give poor families the same opportunities that rich folks have for their children.

Disputing nearly everything about our nation's view of education is a big job! I hope to do that with a mix of science, good humor, anecdote, observation and logic.

There are many women and men fighting for children and for the importance of good, sane, loving education. I intend that within these pages readers will find a perspective, an anecdote, a reference to research, a sentence or a phrase that can help change a policy, support a child, reinforce their own convictions or change their minds. I hope teachers in all schools will find this book a support for the important work they do. Perhaps parents will find this book useful in advocating for their own children, or in demanding a school that nourishes children and does no harm. If so, my modest efforts will be useful.

Chapter One

The Purpose of Education

For more than 100 years the primary purpose of conventional, factory style education has been, borrowing the eloquent Jonathan Kozol's words, to "process" and "finish" children for some future productive use.

As a progressive educator I suggest these as the primary purposes of education:

1. To stir in each child a continuous commitment to be thoughtfully engaged in the ongoing evolution of our democratic republic and to exercise his/her individual and collective responsibilities within the global community.

2. To allow all children to learn and grow into deeply satisfying and ethical lives.

A Continuous Commitment to the World

One of the central tenets of progressive education, particularly as expressed by John Dewey, is its critical role in sustaining our great democratic experiment. In his seminal treatise *The School and Society*, [2] originally a series of lectures, Dewey makes a compelling case for the necessity of progressive education in the care and evolution or our republic. He regarded education as fundamental to a thriving democracy. In The School and Society, Dewey drew a vivid contrast – he argued that a progressive approach, based on curiosity and exploration, leads to critical thinking and powerful ideas. He observed that a mechanistic, rote approach leads to repression, closed minds and conformity. This is, in essence, the difference between education and training. That contrast is at the center of my purposes in writing this book.

The contrasting effects of open-minded education and strict training are often revealed in political and cultural events.

For example, in late February 2015, former New York Mayor Rudy Giuliani raised a ruckus by stating that President Barack Obama didn't love his country. It may seem digressive, but this incident serves as a powerful contemporary example of the difference between unquestioning compliance and lively, loving, critical engagement. Irritated by Giuliani's mean-spirited comments, I wrote this in a newspaper column:

> *The late Reverend William Sloane Coffin, Jr. described his relationship with America as that of a critical lover. I can state with confidence that he would have been deeply troubled by Rudy Giuliani's gratuitous attack on President Obama. As has been widely reported, Giuliani said, "I do*

not believe, and I know this is a horrible thing to say, but I do not believe that the president loves America. He doesn't love you. And he doesn't love me. He wasn't brought up the way you were brought up and I was brought up through love of this country."

The only true phrase in Giuliani's statement is "... this is a horrible thing to say."

Coffin, who lived in Strafford, VT for the last decades of his remarkable life, was my friend and musical partner. While I am not religious, Coffin's inclusive Christianity was sufficiently wide and generous to include me in its embrace.

Perhaps another Coffin perspective is equally powerful in considering the Giuliani iteration of patriotic love. Coffin frequently reminded his friends and followers, "You can't take Scripture seriously if you take it literally." His rejection of Scriptural literalism did not dilute his faith – it was central to his faith. His loving God encompassed both the "better angels of our nature" and the deep flaws of our humanity.

Love of country is thin if left unexamined. The current clash between the President's measured stance and the American Exceptionalism espoused by Giuliani and others is analogous to Coffin's understanding of love and faith. Mindless, uncritical faith, whether in God or country, is far more dangerous than no faith at all.

Patriotism and love of country require constant self-examination. The values and possibilities implicit in the founding of America are remarkably prescient: The balance of powers, the self-perpetuating mechanisms of governance, the ability to amend and revise the Constitution which has guided us through several hundred years of growth and change. We can sustain our promise and our future only through humility and self-criticism.

The notion that Barack Obama doesn't "love America" is preposterous on its face, unless one embraces the delusional conspiracy theory that he is a Muslim Socialist and has ascended to the Presidency as part of a sinister plot. There has been no president in memory who has endured more vitriol in service to his country than Obama. While I have reservations about his politics, wishing he were more consistently progressive, he has weathered the slanderous attacks from his opponents with remarkable grace and dignity. He loves this country enough to retain confidence that it can live up to its ideals, even when it has strayed furthest from them.

As to, "he doesn't love you," this is a president who strives to love all of "you." It is easy to love those who are most like you. The self-adoration on the political right and among rigid conservative evangelicals is evidence of this easy love. Obama has shown no disdain, even for those who have lied about his ancestry, attacked his character, insulted his family, questioned his faith and employed racist epithets to diminish his stature as a man.

And as to Giuliani's "He wasn't brought up the way you were brought up and I was brought up through love of this country." No, Mr. Giuliani, he was not brought up that way. And thank whatever God you worship (or don't) that he was not brought up this way. He was not brought up in an exclusive faith that denies full humanity to women. He was not brought up with unexamined white privilege. He was not brought up to believe poverty is a character flaw and that punishment solves problems.

It has been our great fortune to have a president who retains grace and dignity in the face of hatred. We are lucky to finally have a leader who has experienced the sharp pain of racism and sustained his patient hopes for America despite its flaws.

No, Mr. Giuliani, America needs critical lovers, not angry, opportunistic nationalists. It is you, not he, who repre- sents the real threat to our future. And that, sir, is not a horrible thing to say.

The current state of education as fashioned by so-called reform is more likely to produce blind followers than critical lovers.

The sharpest examples of educating for unquestioning con- formity are the publicly funded religious schools enabled by reform. More than 80% of school vouchers are used to attend religious schools. Given this political reality it is ironic, to say the least, that many of the politicians who support school choice rail against schools like Muslim Madrassas, which have a mix of sectarian and secular purposes, while promoting analogous Christian schools that are nearly indistinguishable from Madrassas in their imposition of religious doctrine and nationalism. Neither promotes critical thought. Both require unquestioning theological compliance. Not all Madrassas are sources of radical anti-American, pro-terrorist doctrine and not all of America's Christian schools are fundamentalist, evangeli- cal, homophobic, anti-evolution, climate-change-denying institutions. But is not misplaced to say that neither Madrassas nor Christian schools are in the business of developing skepticism and critical capacity. They have every right, perhaps in their view divine right, to exist. But not on the taxpayer dime, as they are more likely to rend, not strengthen, the elegant fabric of our democratic republic.

It is important to acknowledge that many of the religious schools now receiving public funds through vouchers are Catholic schools. Many Catholic schools are not fiercely dogmatic or doctrinaire, especially Jesuit schools, but public funding is nevertheless an Establishment Clause violation. Public funding of any religious school violates the First Amendment guarantee of freedom from religion – unless one is convinced that our founders really wanted to establish a Christian nation under God, but just forgot to write it down.

Even in regular public schools, conformity and compliance can take a dangerously nationalistic and exclusive form, like in Texas, where the school board insisted on a white and white-washed version of history, or in New Mexico, where legislators mounted a mean-spirited assault on Mexican-American studies – never mind that we are a nation of immigrants and that the promise of America is its commitment to inclusion not its tarnished history of exclusion and discrimination.

These extreme examples are not the most serious problem. These kinds of schools are relatively small in number and their impact is minor. The more serious problem is the effect of education reform on all public schools. The majority of schools, public or charter, may not engage in jingoism or religious proselytizing, but they surely are not cauldrons for forging a generation of critical lovers of country or open-minded citizens of a global society. Children in most American schools have always been expected, explicitly or implicitly, to conform and comply. This is not new. From Eurocentric curricula to the daily Pledge of Allegiance, conventional public education has always inculcated civic conformity.

As the testing and accountability era has progressed, two phenomena have intensified the expectation of conformity and compliance. Teachers are forced to "teach to the test" because their students' test scores will affect their evaluations, perhaps their careers, and often the viability of their schools. Students are left little choice other than to "learn to the test," whether to survive the testing regimen in an underfunded public school, avoid sanctions or expulsion from a charter school, or assemble luminous credentials to win the college chase from an affluent community or a prestigious private school. Extrinsic structures of accountability and competition erode innate curiosity and punish risk-taking in all schools.

Even the seemingly more benign Common Core drives intellectual conformity and compliance. In a later chapter I offer a tongue-in-cheek critique of a piece of 3rd grade Common Core curriculum and its companion test on maple syrup production. Reducing the fascinating things in life to this kind of dry exercise is bad enough. But the entire Common Core approach supposes that the interpretation of text, the ways to understand mathematical concepts, the "truth" of history, must be among, and only among, the several possible answers presented by the authors of the exam. The world in all its complexity exists only as the architects of the Common Core see it.

The value of a good question rests in the thinking about it, not the answer to it. It's rather like good poetry. When living in Vermont I had the great pleasure of acquaintance with the late Grace Paley, a marvelous poet and short story writer. At a reading in a tiny café in rural Vermont, Grace fielded questions from a small audience of poet wannabees and political progressives who just liked being in her feisty presence. One pretentious looking wannabee in full flax, goatee and beret costume, asked Grace what her poem "meant." She looked piercingly and responded, "I don't know. You decide." While only semi-relevant to this argument, I can't resist another anecdote – another wannabee asked Grace, "What advice do you have for an aspiring poet?" Without skipping a beat she dryly responded, "Keep a low overhead." I'll leave the reader to unpeel the several layers of that tart and brilliant rejoinder.

Democracy is messy. The processes that prepare children to participate in democracy should be messy too. Kids should test their opinions without risk, challenge conventional wisdom, question authority and learn to live passionate, engaged lives.

In Chapter 8, I describe a 6 year-old student at Summerhill, [3] who challenged the school's founder, A.S. Neill, by breaking a window and claiming impunity by virtue of Neill's dictatorship. This student was preparing to be a model citizen. Contrast his experience with a charter school student told to walk silently through the hallways and then, seated with hands folded on the desk, told repeatedly, "Eyes on teacher!"

The way to sustain and advance a democratic, civil society is not to "instruct it." Students should explore democracy and live it. Schools should provide daily practice in democracy, honoring students' points of view, learning from them as they learn from us, absorbing and redirecting the inevitable mistakes they will make as they discover their way into thoughtful citizenship.

An Ethical and Satisfying Life

A deeply satisfying, ethical life is not enabled by the narrow purposes of current educational policy. All the chatter about education, particularly among reformers, is about vocation. In the spring of 2015, Wisconsin Governor and presidential aspirant Scott Walker slyly attempted to revise the University of Wisconsin's historic commitment to the "search for truth," "to educate people and improve the human condition" and "to serve and stimulate society." At the same time that he proposed a $300 million cut to the university system, he offered a new mission – higher education exists to serve "the state's work force needs." Walker backed away from this mission change, but the shift in American education from intellectual to vocational is relentless.

It isn't that vocation is trivial. We must all find a way to make our way in the world, to pay the bills, be responsible, and to contribute to the incredibly complex matrix of economic activity that sustains a society. But these pragmatic concerns should be secondary, not primary.

The vast majority of people I've known in my lifetime derive the greatest satisfaction from things outside their work. The number of Americans who report satisfaction with their jobs has steadily declined from 61% in 1987 to 42.6% in 2010, according to the Conference Board, a New York-based non-profit research group. [4] And satisfaction with a job tends to mean only that work is not exploitive, abusive or tedious. Even those who report that they "love" their jobs often mean, "I love my work more than some other work that I could be saddled with, or the really lousy job I used to have." And, among the minority who are satisfied with their jobs, often the most positive aspect of the job is the people with whom they work, not the work itself. Much ed-reform rhetoric is about preparing students with "21st century skills." In the next breath comes the ironic and contradictory acknowledgement that we haven't the faintest idea what those 21st century skills might be in five years, or even next month. If we limit education to vocational preparation as the uniform factory model aspires to do, one thing is certain – that preparation will be obsolete long before a toddler reaches puberty.

A progressive understanding of the purpose of education is grounded in the conviction that each child is filled with limitless potential. As expressed so beautifully by psychologist Wendy Mogel, [5] each child is a wildflower seed in an unmarked package, needing only water, patience and the warmth of the sun to draw out her beauty. This natural process can be enhanced or inhibited in school environments. The contemporary version of conventional education, particularly in this "reform" era, is doing little enhancing and a lot of inhibiting.

Among life's greatest satisfaction are relationships, successful, intimate partnerships, children, grandchildren and friendships. At first glance, these things may appear to have little to do with school, whether conventional or progressive. But consider the worst aspects of conventional education – does a rigid, authoritarian charter school environment nurture the empathy, compassion and warmth that characterize deeply satisfying relationships? Does immersion in test-driven competition encourage the cooperation, collaboration and selflessness that make great partnerships? Do the examples set by "no excuses" and "tough love" schools augur well for loving and nurturing parenting or grandparenting?

What are the childhood experiences that offer the possibility of a satisfying life? Because of privilege I was regularly exposed to beautiful music and its effect on my life has been profound. Our home was filled with art, games, puzzles, irreverence and reverence. I read books because I was free to read whatever I wanted, and I didn't have hours of homework every night (or when I did, I didn't always do it). I had the time and space to explore endlessly, and thus love wilderness and natural phenomena of all kinds. I was free to be silly, curious, aimless, ambitious, risky, irresponsible and romantic. The inadequacies of my education were fairly benign. I suppose I was born on second base, but I have never thought I hit a double.

Many children are not so lucky. Particularly in the poorest neighborhoods, school may be the only place children are exposed to the things that might provide a lifetime of satisfaction – love of music, art and great literature, playing an instrument, fascination with the natural world through trips to parks and caring for creatures in the science room, exposure to worlds far beyond the neighborhood, exciting the imagination and creating a great urge to travel and learn. These are things many people of privilege take for granted.

This self-reference is offered as a mirror for the privileged folks who drive the very conventional education reform movement, hoping they'll catch a glimpse of self. The experiences their privilege has provided account in part for their success and their access to power and influence. I wish reformers were more interested in providing poor children with middle class experiences like their own, rather than bootstraps to pull.

I suspect this is the reason there aren't more people concerned about the flaws in conventional education. Most of those who support conventional education through policy, practice, parenting, or politics, are people who fared reasonably well in conventional schools and who enjoyed the benefits of middle or upper middle class comfort, thereby having no urgent motivation to examine the issues raised in this book. It's a bit like healthy people with good insurance having no urgent motivation to support universal health care.

But I didn't write this book for lucky people. I wrote it on behalf of everyone else. School is often – too often – the only place children might experience the joy of a good story, express an unusual point of view, create something original or discover a life's passion. For the least privileged children in America, "school choice" is really a Sophie's Choice between a bleak, enervating, underfunded public school or a rigid, highly programmed charter school with strict emphasis on conformity and compliance.

One of the declared intentions of education reform is to break the cycle of poverty by reducing the achievement gap between white and black, privileged and poor. All of the evidence indicates that it isn't working. It can't work well, given the flawed neurobiological and psychological premises on which reform is based. But even if the grit and drill *were* resulting in higher test scores, the toll on children is far too great. In the majority of today's schools, children are seldom introduced to beauty, they only read stories so they can answer multiple choice questions, they are infrequently invited or allowed to express a point of view, they are bound by the conventional, not encouraged toward the original, and their passion is suppressed, or sometimes even punished. With long school hours, long school years and long hours of homework, they have less time for play and pleasure than most of the adults who place these heavy loads on their shoulders.

If you share my belief that education should draw children into deeply satisfying and ethical lives, then this is certainly not the direction we've taken, especially for poor children. When I think of the richness of my own life, my children's lives, and my grandchildren's lives, I am infuriated at the images of small brown and black children marching silently through school, grinding toward the next stressful test.

Chapter Two

How Did We Get Here?

A Very Short History of Progressive Education

The case for a progressive approach to education cannot be made without historical context. Usually when the term "progressive" is contrasted with the term "traditional" it constitutes a profound misunderstanding of both terms.

As progressive educator Alfie Kohn and others point out, traditional education is the newcomer, largely an industrial, mechanistic approach that took hold in the early 20th century. Most aspects of progressive education have centuries-old roots. The 20th and 21st century dominance of traditional education is a political and economic phenomenon, not a product of enlightenment. The central principles of progressive education arise from the steady evolution of understanding human development. Many historians have traced this lineage more thoroughly than I intend, but this historical perspective is important in order to understand the dismal state of education today. For the reason Kohn cites, I use the term "conventional" rather than "traditional" throughout this text, since the word "traditional" confers an undeserved historical gravitas.

Aspects of a progressive approach are apparent from earliest recorded history. Aphorisms about learning and education abound:

"I cannot teach anybody anything; I can only make them think." – Socrates

"You cannot teach a man anything; you can only help him discover it in himself." – Galileo

"Educating the mind without educating the heart is no education at all." – Aristotle

"I hear and I forget, I see and I remember. I do and I understand." – Chinese proverb

Beginning in the 18th century a series of philosophers, psychologists and educators began forming the more contemporary iteration of progressive theory. At the risk of oversimplification, the central notion of this new way of educating was to recognize and respond to the natural development of children.

Among the earliest and most prominent "parents" of progressive education was Swiss-born Johann Heinrich Pestalozzi (1746-1827). Pestalozzi recognized the inextricable connections between "Head, Heart and Hand." He was among the earliest theorists to write of child-centered education and the importance of individual differences. In view of our current understanding of child development, multiple intelligences and neurobiology, his prescience was astounding. It is even more astounding that 250 years later, our national education policies are not mindful of the human realities he observed and described.

Pestalozzi's most famous student, the German Friedrich Froebel (1782-1852), created the notion of kindergarten (and coined the word). Froebel, like his mentor, recognized the developmental importance of play and offered the world "Froebel Gifts," the first organized materials based on learning through play. As with Pestalozzi, he spawned many disciples, most notably Margarethe Schurz (1833-1876), who founded America's first kindergarten, in Wisconsin. Other Froebel students founded kindergarten programs in Boston and New York City.

Better known within and beyond education circles are Maria Montessori and Jean Piaget.

The Italian Montesorri (1870-1952), in whose name an international collection of schools thrives today, continued and advanced the progressive approach to children and learning. She too observed the natural development of children and was a powerful proponent of student choice. She pioneered the practice of organizing children in mixed age groups. Many schools, notably the Bank Street School in New York City, mix children of different ages in learning groups despite the cultural resistance such practices draw. Montessori also advocated longer, uninterrupted blocks of time and she urged educators to "refrain from obtrusive interference." Block scheduling and student choice are hallmarks of most contemporary progressive schools.

Jean Piaget (1896-1980), a Swiss psychologist and philosopher, is considered the pioneer of a constructivist theory of knowing. Most undergraduate psychology students learned his sequential stages of child cognitive development – sensorimotor, pre-operational, concrete operational, formal operational, and abstract thinking. As is true with his predecessors, Piaget's propositions, formed through observation, experimentation and intuition, have proven remarkably prescient.

Inspired by this growing body of knowledge, progressive schools flourished in the late 19th century, particularly in Europe. The King Alfred School in London, where I spent a few enjoyable days in 2009, spawned A.S. Neill's famous Summerhill School, to which I will refer in more detail later in Chapter 8.

Several other progressive schools inspired worldwide emulation, including the Waldorf Schools, based on the educational philosophy of Rudolf Steiner (1861-1925), an Austrian philosopher and social reformer. Waldorf or Steiner schools thrive in nearly every part of the United States.

During the 1890's and early in the 20th century progressive schools took hold in the United States, influenced most notably by American philosopher John Dewey (1859-1952) and Francis Parker (1837-1902). For a short time Dewey's children attended Parker's school in Chicago. Parker and Dewey are widely considered primary influences in the American progressive movement. They both championed learning through activity, project-based pedagogy, the view that schools and students are agents for social change, and the rejection of a rote, mechanistic, authoritarian approach to education. Their influence and schools bearing their names persist despite the current anti-progressive climate.

In New York, Felix Adler (1851-1933) started the Workingman's School in 1878, a tuition-free school for the children of working people, which became the Ethical Culture School shortly thereafter and is now known as the Ethical Culture Fieldston School. The progressive Helen Parkhurst (1887-1973) developed the Dalton Plan, a feature of the Dalton School in Manhattan. There are many other progressive schools around America that arose during this era, although many are now defunct. Sadly, many of these formerly progressive schools have succumbed to a conventional misunderstanding of education and drifted away from progressive philosophy and practice.

Another manifestation of progressive theory is seen in the Reggio Emilia Approach. This philosophy of child development and learning arose in Italy in the aftermath of World War II. Reggio Emilia is not the name of a person, but the name of a village in and around which schools were developed by Loris Malaguzzi (1945-1993), a teacher who was deeply influenced by the progressive theorists of the 18th and 19th centuries. The Reggio Emilia philosophy continues to influence progressive schools around the world.

As the 20th century progressed, many philosophers and educational theorists added to and amended the work of these early progressives. While dozens could be noted, I specifically cite Lev Vygotsky, Jerome Bruner and Howard Gardner.

The Russian psychologist Lev Vygotsky (1896-1934) is perhaps best known for his notion of the Zone of Proximal Development (ZPD). This concept is rightly credited with influencing the educational concept of scaffolding. Scaffolding, over-simply stated, is the layered sequence of experiences, support and materials that draw children through the stages of cognitive development. As I intend no academic treatise, readers may wish to explore Vygotsky in more detail, as his contributions to educational theory are a critical part of the evolution of a progressive approach to learning.

New York-born psychologist Jerome Bruner (1915-2016) is widely considered one of the founders of cognitive psychology. Like Vygotsky, he was instrumental in developing the idea of scaffolding. He was also acutely aware of learning as a social experience, describing the importance of relationships and interaction to the construction of knowledge and, particularly, increasingly sophisticated language acquisition.

Bruner was advisor to Presidents Kennedy and Johnson, quite likely as a result of his book, *The Process of Education.* [6] Therein he wrote, "Knowing how something is put together is worth a thousand facts about it." Perhaps no single sentence better captures the essential contrast between a progressive education and the facts-based approach to schools that infects the majority of schools in America today.

Finally, a short history of progressive education would be remiss if neglecting the work of Howard Gardner (1943-present), Harvard Professor and Senior Director of Harvard Project Zero. A more comprehensive summary of his contributions to cognition and education is in Chapter 5. Most notably, four of his books, taken in sequence, should have inalterably changed the course of American education. The first of these three, published in 1973, is *The Arts and Human Development.* [7] This seminal text explicates the powerful role of the arts in all of recorded history, and begins a career-long examination of the development of the creative process in humans. In *The Arts and Human Development* he posits that previous work in cognitive and developmental psychology, particularly Piaget's theoretical propositions, attended only to the logical/scientific realm of human learning and performance. He suggested that the artistic/creative potential and development had been given (and is still given) too little attention.

In 1983 he published *Frames of Mind: The Theory of Multiple Intelligences*. [8] This groundbreaking work proposed that our dualistic view of intelligence (linguistic and logical-mathematical) was gravely insufficient. He proposed 5 other ways in which humans are intelligent musical – rhythmic, visual-spatial, bodily-kinesthetic, interpersonal and intrapersonal. In later years he proposed that naturalistic and existential intelligences be added to the inventory.

In 1993, in the midst of another policy juncture, Gardner published *Multiple Intelligences: The Theory in Practice*. [9] This should have served as a clarion call to education reformers, much as the early progressive theorists provided in the late 19th and early 20th centuries, but once again a conventional, mechanistic approach prevailed in political and policy circles. We have paid a heavy price thereafter.

His work continues to have great relevance to education. As discussed in Chapter 5, attending only or primarily to linguistic and mathematical intelligence is educational neglect. Yet that is what most schools do today.

This somewhat selective and abbreviated version of the history of progressive education is offered only to disabuse those who think progressive education is the evil, permissive spawn of 1960's hippies. Quite to the contrary, contemporary progressive theory and practice is the product of several hundred years of intellectual and scientific progress. That's why it's called "progress"ive!

It is at significant peril that we ignore the cumulative wisdom inherent in this legacy. It would be like designing a biology curriculum without any regard to the theory of evolution. Oh, wait …

But Didn't We Try That Already?

In a word, "No."

Conventional wisdom, or what passes for wisdom among many folks, is that the progressive era of the late '60s and early '70s ruined virtually everything. Moral values disappeared in a haze of marijuana smoke. Highly sexualized music and an epidemic of free love led to a decline in marriage and erosion of family values. Progressive political values created a spineless, dependent populace, which accounts for the tens of millions of feckless "takers" who look to the nanny state for care and feeding.

And permissive progressive education created a generation of self-indulgent brats who were told everything they did was right when, in fact, they didn't learn anything at all. This misrepresentation of progressive education suggests that child-centered means spoiling children, that self-esteem means every child gets a trophy, and that in progressive schools the teachers wear Birkenstocks and flax shawls and smoke weed as their students run wild and barefoot. This caricature is often advanced by folks who seem to have lingering resentment over the "sex, drugs and rock 'n' roll" era. (I've always suspected that their resentment lingers in part because they didn't get enough of those things.)

There are many problems with this narrative, foremost of

which is that none of it happened, at least not to an important extent.

As a veteran of the '60s, I testify from experience. The vast majority of young folks who joined the counter-culture, wore bell bottoms, smoked weed, went to Woodstock and protested the war, were no more genuine than Justin Bieber wearing saggin' pants, lots of bling and a big brimmed cap on sideways. Most hippies were no more Che Guevara than Bieber is 50 Cent. It was almost all costume and fad or, to use a more current quip, all hat and no cattle.

I attended many anti-war demonstrations in the late '60s and early '70s and most protestors couldn't even find Vietnam on a map! In my middle/upper middle class community, many bra-less girls and bell-bottomed boys had been Brownies and Cub Scouts a few years earlier, and would be aspiring bankers and real estate agents a few years later. At the core there were, as now, small numbers of deeply committed activists, but the majority of folks were along for the ride – and it was a fine trip!

But the bigger lie is that the progressive educational practices of the '60s and '70s eviscerated standards and account for the allegedly miserable state of education today. So-called reformers want rigid accountability, more structure, longer school days, longer school years, more tests and more discipline. Undoing the damage of those loosey-goosey progressive practices is arduous work!

That didn't happen either.

The real progressive movement in education was in the late 19th and early 20th century, when progressive and radical schools in North America and Europe were waging war with the factory model of education promulgated by Ellwood Cubberley (1868-1941), John Franklin Bobbitt (1876-1956) and others.

Edward L. Thorndike (1874-1949), who taught at Columbia University's Teachers College during the progressive John Dewey's tenure, was arguably the single individual who most influenced this shift away from progressive. Thorndike's research led him to propose a stimulus-response definition of intelligence that sparked the spread of worker training through vocational-style education. This narrow conception of intelligence repudiated progressive ideas about the connection between thinking and doing. The truth is that progressive lost and factory won. Progressives have been fighting an uphill battle against a factory/business model ever since.

There was a brief flurry of progressive activity in the '60s and '70s, when some schools adopted open floor plans and a few humanistic and humane programs poked through the dull homogeneity of public education. Most schools were designed in spirit-numbing form, and curriculum and pedagogy trudged along in the same rote, uninspiring way.

Here too I'm a veteran and I testify as both participant and witness. I graduated high school in 1964. My younger brother went to the same schools in the late '60s and '70s. I had children early and my daughter began school in the same community in 1975, my son three years later. That's pretty good coverage of the alleged progressive era. All of this happened in one of America's most progressive suburban communities (Cleveland Heights, Ohio). Progressive education never happened there … or most anywhere around the country.

The factory model of education never intended that children be truly educated. It aspired then, and now, to train children in a set of skills that will allow them to be productive workers. That's a pretty barren way to look at children, but if you listen between the lines of the rhetoric of today's so-called educational reformers, it is precisely what they seek.

For more than a century, progressive education has been relegated to the fringes as mechanistic, industrial style schools have dominated. The 21st century iteration of conventional education is particularly virulent. It is not hyperbole to suggest that millions of American children might be better served to skip school entirely. The policies and practices in some schools, particularly those in the least privileged and most privileged neighborhoods, are not merely ineffective – they are harmful.

We humans have a remarkable capacity to ignore what we know and act stupidly – the United States Congress and climate change comes to mind. But even considering that breathtaking (literally) phrase, education stands apart as the field where "what we do" most violently clashes with "what we know." Steady advances in our understanding of child development, neurobiology and psychology have confirmed what progressive educators have known for several centuries.

My 18 years of work in a progressive school have led to the realization that most folks have a very conventional view of education. Convincing people of anything new or counter-intuitive (or progressive) in education is an interesting challenge because education is one field where nearly everyone is an expert – because they had one. Most people believe their education worked just fine, even if they didn't like it very much. Those folks tend to be convinced that you're not supposed to like it very much – "no pain, no gain." Individuals for whom education was an unmitigated disaster are nearly invariably led to believe it was their own fault. They were not bright enough or they were not motivated enough.

Minds are hard to change, as most people will go to great lengths to defend their experience or opinion, even in the face of what should be overwhelming evidence to the contrary. I suppose some people will read this book and still hold fast to their conventional view of education.

But if you invite a bit of honest reflection, most people will also recognize what they value and what experiences were important to them. The values and experiences people report are essentially the values and principles of progressive education. So, on one level folks know better, but they still tend to choose sterile, conventional and often unpleasant experiences for their children.

Some years ago I was beginning an admissions presentation to anxious Manhattan parents of potential pre-school applicants. I can't recall what impulse led me to do so, but I interrupted my usual remarks by asking the surprised parents, "Without thinking too hard, would you please identify, in one word, qualities you admire in other humans that you would like to see developed in your children." After only a moment the impromptu responses began. "Curiosity." "Compassion." "Imagination." "Humor." "Creativity." "Integrity." "Empathy." "Originality." "Courage." "Honesty." When the torrent slowed I asked, "Don't you find it odd that very few of the qualities you most admire are intentionally nurtured in schools? In fact," I continued, "many of these things are suppressed or, worse, punished in many schools. Some of you may choose schools like that."

Emboldened by the endorsement of all the things my progressive school intends, I pressed my luck. "Now, think a little harder and conjure up one educational experience in your own life, any time from nursery school to post-graduate work, that you recall as powerful and important."

The anecdotes poured out. Teachers remembered fondly for long digressions from the dull syllabus. Blowing things up in 2nd grade. The first time a teacher recognized a special talent within error-ridden prose. A life-changing trip. A chance to be a leader. Building something. A simulation that brought history or literature into vivid, highly personal, context. The simple experience of being noticed and loved without judgment. As I observed with good humor, no parent affectionately recalled a vocabulary test, dozens of math worksheets, long nights of cramming for mid-term exams, or the joys of SAT preparation. Keep in mind that I did not ask them to recall the times they had the most fun in school. I asked what things were most powerful and important to them.

I suspect readers are now recalling some of their own important and powerful learning experiences. If some tedious, stressful, memorization task comes to mind, stop reading and give this book to a friend.

That these powerful and important experiences were often fun is not coincidental. We have been culturally conditioned to believe that learning is supposed to be hard, even unpleasant. No pain, no gain. Rigor, rigor, rigor. (It bears noting that the word "rigor" is most frequently paired with "mortis.") In the service of preparing young folks for their productive place in the global economy we have turned schools into grim factories (albeit with colorful banners and faux enthusiasm) with ever-longer schooldays and school years and mountains of suffocating homework.

Given this cultural misunderstanding many parents believe they face a difficult choice. Shall I surrender my child to years of hard labor so that she will have a successful life? Or shall I allow her to daydream, play with friends, read fantastic books, and sentence her to live at home for the rest of her life? Of course some of us think daydreaming, playing with friends and reading fantastic books *are* a successful life. I'm 69 and still think that. But that's not the point.

It's a false choice. Daydreaming, playing, fantasy, and friends are also the ingredients that make successful doctors, lawyers, scientists, social workers, hedge fund managers, architects, Nobel Prize winners, and poets. From both a psychological and neurobiological point of view, long hours of homework, Advanced Placement tests and other elements of so-called high achievement, may actually reduce the possibility of conspicuous achievement – if it is conspicuous achievement that you value.

Another glaring disconnect in the current view of education is found in political rhetoric. Most of the frothing, on both sides of the political aisle, compares our kids to the kids in places like Shanghai or South Korea, pointing out that they are eating our lunch on international measures like the Programme for International Student Assessment (PISA) tests. This is not true, but "truth" does not thrive in political circles. I'll dispense with this issue briefly, leaving the reader free to peruse other sources that more fully explicate the bad science involved. Diane Ravitch, for example, deals with this astutely in her wonderful book, *Reign of Error: The Hoax of the Privatization Movement and the Danger to America's Public Schools.* [10]

PISA tests are taken by highly varied pools of kids from one country to another, thus rendering any comparative analysis moot, and the tests don't measure anything important anyway. But here's a dazzling irony – while American politicians and pundits suffer PISA envy, the nations they admire are increasingly aware of the flaws of their very conventional approaches and are turning to progressive philosophy to make education more meaningful.

Among those debunking the myth of Asian superiority, Yong Zhao stands tall. A scholar at the University of Oregon, Zhao's book, *Who's Afraid of the Big Bad Dragon: Why China has the Best (and Worst) Education System in the World*, [11] summarizes the deep inadequacies of the Chinese system, which indeed produces good test scores, but at the expense of innovation, critical capacities, creativity, imagination, and problem solving. He is among many Asians and Asian Americans who wish education, in China and South Korea for example, would take a more progressive turn.

In 2014 I had several experiences that revealed this counterintuitive trend. A group of early childhood educators from China were sent by their government to explore how American schools, particularly progressive schools, design programs for early childhood. During their visit to Calhoun their hunger for a more human, humane and developmentally appropriate approach was palpable. They toured our open, joyful spaces with great curiosity and an hour-long meeting in my office revealed their great interest in developing play-based, progressive practices in their Chinese schools.

Later in the year I was invited to speak about progressive education to 30 Chinese university students visiting the United States. They were apparently among the best of the best, thus selected for this program. I recounted the experience in a blog post:

I entered the NYU classroom to a respectful round of applause. The clapping ended abruptly and there I stood, staring at 30 expressionless faces, young women and men sitting at desks in neat rows, all dressed similarly. The casual banter I usually use to relax a group was like pulling teeth. I finally drew a forced smile or two and learned that this was the first visit to the United States for all of them.

A progressive approach to education is hard enough to explain to a group of Manhattan parents. Here, I thought, language and cultural barriers would make my philosophical, neurobiological, psychological and educational musings sound like utter gibberish. (Which is also how some Manhattan parents hear it!)

But I forged earnestly ahead, as I couldn't think of anything better to present that wouldn't be equally opaque. I talked about Dewey, Froebel, Pestalozzi, Montessori, John Holt and Howard Gardner. I raged against rote learning, cited the abuse of long hours of tedious homework, railed against No Child Left Behind, pointed out that grade-level expectations are crazy when children are not level, argued that humans learn best through experience, ranted about the importance of play. I tried to moderate my cadence to meet their language skills, whatever they were. Now and then I would interject, "Are you understanding this?" and receive a very tentative nod here and there.

I rather critically, apologetically and respectfully alluded to what I believed to be problems with the Chinese system.

A nod here and there. I acknowledged that I was free to criticize China and they might be less so. Only one nod. Finally, when I emphasized a point by dancing like a fool, I got a few wide smiles. By the 40-minute mark the room was noticeably looser.

Just short of the hour limit, I opened the room to questions, fairly sure there would be few or none. A hand went up.

As with all subsequent questioners, this young man rose respectfully to his feet. "I completely support everything you've said, but are these things possible in the larger classes that are necessary in China?" Whew, I thought, this guy really was listening and listening well.

"As you said, Mr. Nelson, the Chinese system shuts off opportunity for many children who don't do well on tests in early years. What can we do to keep dreams alive for children who lose hope at 11 or 12?"

"If I were appointed Minister of Education for China tomorrow, what would you suggest as the very first thing I should do?"

"I very much support progressive education, but we have a long cultural history that makes it difficult to make such change."

At about this time I reminded them that my school uses first names and they should call me Steve. The next questioner blushed, giggled nervously and started, "Steve ... "This small shift transformed the room. Questions were delivered with warmth and trust. Smiles abounded.

Space precludes a full description of the 45 minutes that followed, but it was simply remarkable. They had a very deep understanding of the severe limits and inequity of the very system within which they had succeeded. It could have lasted hours longer. When I finally got ready to leave there were the typical ceremonial pictures. All the formality was gone. I got several hugs.

As I left, a chorus of 30 liberated voices shouted, "Bye Steve!!" That afternoon may have been the first time any of them called a 'teacher' by first name. Just before I turned down the hall to the elevator, the young man who had been my first smile of the day grabbed my elbow. "I must tell you something."

"Yes?" I asked.

"I have one very important wish. I want to be 3 years old again and start over in a progressive school like yours."

It is amusing that American politicians and so-called reformers talk about how we have to catch up with the Chinese and others, while the Chinese and others are finally coming to their senses and hoping to be more like us – or at least the way they think we are. I don't delude myself into thinking that my lovely encounter with 30 Chinese university students portends a seismic shift in Chinese policy, but it is a clear indication of the universal desire for real, human, humane – yes, progressive – education, even among those who can only dream about starting over.

But beyond the "falling behind the rest of the world" rhetoric, the inconsistency between what we Americans say and what we do peaks when education reformers talk about America's greatest needs. Policy makers and politicians cite the need for:

- *Entrepreneurs and innovators* - then they drive sterile policies and practices that have children completing worksheets, complying with teachers' directions, sitting silently, respecting their elders;

- *Problem solvers* - then they adopt policies that train children to get the answers right on a test, punishing any risk taking or original thinking;

- *Leaders* - then they design systems that reward kids only when they blindly follow;

- *Visionaries* - but they don't have time to hear children's ideas.

They use trite phrases like "thinks outside the box" to describe qualities they admire, and then present children with boxes to check and scold them for coloring outside the lines.

Despite the fact that I am an incurable romantic, I understand that education has its practical benefits. Literacy and a basic knowledge of mathematics and science are prerequisites for many vocations. Skills and information may be necessary, but they are gravely insufficient. In the unnecessarily exclusive service of these modest ambitions we have driven the much more noble purposes of education out of schools. Schools should be where all children construct their own sense of the world and their place in it. Education should cultivate the capacity to recognize and create beauty. School is a place where empathy and compassion should be honored and developed. The flames of curiosity should be fanned, not smothered. Skepticism should be sharply honed.

Perhaps the greatest sin of much current educational practice is that it robs children of their childhood. An example of the saddest manifestation of this is described in Jonathan Kozol's powerful and important book, *Ordinary Resurrections: Children in the Years of Hope.* [12] Kozol describes the lives of children in the Mott Haven neighborhood of the Bronx. He rails with dignified eloquence against policies and practices that treat poor children as fodder to be prepared for some future economic use. He describes Mariposa, a small child of color in the neighborhood:

> *Mariposa is not simply thirty-seven pounds of raw material that wants a certain 'processing' and 'finishing' before she can be shipped to market and considered to have value. She is of value now, and if she dies of a disease or accident when she is 12 years old, the sixth year of her life will not as a result be robbed of meaning.*

Kozol's poignant indignation takes into account the sad possibility that her life is more likely to end abruptly than the lives of children of privilege. But I intend much more than that. One cannot know whether a 6 year-old child is likely, as a result of the deck stacked against her, to be robbed of many years. But all 6 year-old children are alive today and their lives are important. They are as or more vibrantly alive than you or I, and they deserve unfettered time to do the things that bring meaning and joy to their lives. "Processing" and "finishing" for future use should not be a primary aim.

This notion is important in the lives of children of privilege too. For far too many children of privilege, the spaces in which they might daydream, build a magical structure or learn to negotiate the playground are filled with adult-structured time that denies them the experiences they most need and enjoy. It is a high-class version of processing and finishing and it should also be viewed with concern, albeit a small rash compared to the gaping wounds caused by poverty and racism.

In and out of school, children (and adults) need time to be reflective, to daydream, to consolidate memories, to imagine and create. Seeds of brilliance need a dose of aimlessness to flower. In all art forms, the most profound work sometimes emerges from near-sloth. Poets and composers often speak of the poem or melody that "came to them" only when the clutter was removed from daily existence. Mathematicians and philosophers seldom develop seminal insights through highly structured, intense work. "I want a brilliant theory on my desk in 30 minutes!" I don't think so. These things often arise from empty space and silence, from stretches of indulgent, seemingly aimless musing – walks in the woods, long stretches of solitude. The muse arrives only when all the obligatory invited guests have departed.

This experience is not exclusive to artists and scholars. Innovations of all kinds, in business, technology, science and other fields, don't automatically come under the pressure of deadlines. They often emerge when the conscious, the subconscious, intuition and knowledge are given room to merge in alchemical bloom. For too many students, time is so intensely structured during and after school that creativity and originality don't have time to gestate. Educators and parents should make room for some aimlessness.

Whatever one may believe the purpose of education, the collateral effect need not be the loss of childhood. During the school years, we humans are most vividly alive. It is abusive to make these years drudgery. Children should sing joyfully, laugh at butt jokes, fall in and out of love, experience thrilling adventures, build weird structures, and make up tall tales (or build tall structures and make up weird tales). And those are just the things they should do in school!

We Should Know Better By Now

How did a particularly aggressive iteration of the factory-style of training achieve dominance in the 21st century? Propaganda and money.

The contemporary manifestation of propaganda began with a 1983 report commissioned by the Reagan administration, *A Nation at Risk: The Imperative for Educational Reform*. [13] This report claimed to provide evidence that a deteriorating educational system was undermining America's vitality. It was a big lie, exposed by more honest work in subsequent years, particularly the Sandia Report commissioned in 1990. [14] This subsequent work received little fanfare and nothing changed. Education reform in 2016 is based on the same big lie in new clothing. It has been a 33-year war on public education, teachers and teachers unions. It seems all of America believes that our schools are bad and that education reform is a critical need.

A Nation at Risk appeared to provide unassailable statistical proof that student achievement had dropped. The average scores the report cited were not fiction. They were lower. But it didn't mean what the report concluded.

The 1990 Sandia Report found seemingly contradictory facts. The average test scores of all American students had gone down, as *A Nation at Risk* claimed, but the average test scores of every single sub-group (by class, race, and every other variable) of American students had gone up! How can that be? Enter Simpson's Paradox, a simple and fascinating statistical phenomenon.

To illustrate:

10 students in subgroup A each scored 80 points.

10 students in subgroup B each scored 60 points.

10 students in subgroup C each scored 40 points.

Average score = 60 (1,800 points divided by 30 students).

Change the subgroup size:

10 students in subgroup A each scored 85.

20 students in subgroup B each scored 65.

30 students in subgroup C each scored 45.

Average score = 58.3 (3,500 divided by 60 students).

The overall average dropped from 60 to 58.3 yet every student group actually improved by 6 to 12%!

This is essentially what happened in America. Population growth and increased student enrollment in less privileged communities changed the relative sizes of groups by race and class. But the achievement of every group, including the poorest kids, went up.

The same thing is true in 2016. Politicians and reformers cite poor results on tests, particularly the so-called gold standard, the National Assessment of Educational Progress (NAEP), and the Programme for International Student Assessment (PISA). In both cases, a Simpson's Paradox examination reveals that each subgroup of students in America is doing slightly better than before. We just have more poverty and income inequality, so the subgroups have continued to shift in size as in the illustration above.

The costs of this lie are enormous too. The ill-considered No Child Left Behind law left schools and children in test-stress tatters. Hundreds of millions of dollars have been wasted on tests, test preparation, Common Core, and other medicine for a disease that has been misdiagnosed. America's most shameful problems are racism, poverty and inequality, not teacher unions or insufficient testing.

Beneath the waves of reform, the economic analyses and all the political rhetoric, rests an iceberg of money and influence. What is now happening in education reform is analogous to the broader political process where, for example, forces like the Koch brothers and their grandiose sounding American Legislative Exchange Council (ALEC) have an extraordinary megaphone. They have spawned an astounding number of "think tanks," supposedly non-partisan organizations and other entities, that support their political agenda. ALEC writes sample legislation that state legislatures often pass verbatim.

The same thing is happening in education reform. Education Trust, Democrats for Education Reform, National School Choice Week, Education Post, Students First, Teach for America, Teach Plus, Knowledge is Power Program (KIPP), National Alliance for Public Charter Schools, and dozens more organizations are funded by a coalition of private foundations that is dominating the national conversation. Primary among them are The Bill and Melinda Gates Foundation, the Broad Foundation and the Walton Family Foundation. Much propaganda is produced by these not-for-profit organizations. Many of the organizations are intentionally opaque, but some digging reveals the same deep pockets behind the screen.

Diane Ravitch has exposed this influence in great detail, [10] as has Mercedes Schneider in her important book, *Chronicle of Echoes: Who's Who in the Implosion of Public Education in America.* [15]

In *The Educator And The Oligarch*, [16] Anthony Cody challenges the Gates Foundation's chosen path of data-driven reform, centered on high stakes tests, educational technology and market-based competition between schools. He raises disturbing questions about the growing role corporate philanthropies such as the Gates Foundation are playing in public policy, and the dangers we face when market forces are made central to our educational system.

In *Save Our Children Save Our School*, [17] a political satire, Denny Taylor exposes the political skullduggery, nefarious practices, avarice, and greed behind the corporate coup d'état that is dismantling the US public school system, destroying democracy, and threatening the present and future lives of our children.

I spend at least several hours every week reading about the conflict over education reform. It is as fascinating as it is important. The forces amassed on each side are growing in size and much of the rhetoric is heated. I suppose many on the education reform side will find this book somewhat strident.

That isn't my intent. When I report things like the disciplinary philosophy at KIPP or Democracy Prep, it is out of concern for children, not out of malice for the founders, supporters or teachers. I suppose many reformers are doing what they think is right or, sadly, what they think is necessary.

Many critics accuse reformers of being in it for the money. There is surely plenty of collateral profit to be made. I receive dozens of emails every day, like one I copy verbatim from Pearson in Chapter 3. Hundreds of technology entrepreneurs are capitalizing on reform – creating Common Core applications, test preparation materials, Common Core curriculum, tutoring services, or other programs designed to capture a share of the $700 billion market. Large charter management organizations are not doing the work for the betterment of humankind. A lot of money is being spent on education reform and it is enriching some folks, to be sure.

But what about Bill and Melinda Gates, Eli Broad, the Walton family members or other extremely wealthy folks who are the real forces behind educational reform? When assessing the interlocking pieces of the funding puzzle, as Mercedes Schneider has done so well, it is clear that the reform movement would be relatively toothless without their support. But there is no reasonable evidence to support the idea that they engage in this work to profit.

So what moves them? They claim to do the work because they want to help lift poor children out of poverty and give them an escape route from failing schools. I have no right to doubt the sincerity of that motive. Unfortunately, that sentiment hasn't been returned in kind. Education reform folks have gotten very angry with me, characterizing me – accurately – as the head of an expensive private school, thereby implying that I am disqualified from the debate. I might argue that my position as the head of a private school provides some immunity against accusations of self-interest. Goodness knows I have nothing to gain. I also have nothing to lose.

My sense, particularly when reading the sharp, frustrated tone of reformers' responses to criticism, is that they honestly believe they know what is best. Beginning in the '50s and '60s, America has steadily moved away from intellectualism and toward business-focused pragmatism. Along with the rejection of idealism and intellectualism came a constant imperative to "run things like a business" and "focus on the bottom line." The Reagan-era emphasis on free markets produced an increased adulation of wealth. While it is not entirely a phenomenon of the 20th and 21st centuries, the nearly automatic pairing of money and wisdom is built into our culture. In the late 1980s when I was the president of a performing arts school in Detroit, I experienced this first hand. I suspect most non-profit leaders could tell a similar story.

Members of the Ford family dominated the board of the organization. Some Detroit residents might know that there are "automobile Fords" and "chemical Fords," But they were separate families, and we had both on the board, some of them products of Ford-Ford marriages. Most of these folks were kind and generous. Their support helped provide wonderful music and dance programs to thousands of kids, many quite poor. I remain grateful, all these years later. But the unconscious assumed relationship between wealth and wisdom was revealed in the meetings of the board. The wealthier "auto Fords" were invariably deferred to by the less affluent "chemical Fords." If that dynamic was amusing – and it was – then the relationship between "auto Fords" and "developer Taubman" was hilarious.

A. Alfred Taubman, who died in 2015, made a fortune, mostly by developing upscale shopping malls. He subsequently bought Sotheby's and was briefly incarcerated for a price-fixing scandal. Forbes estimated his net worth at $3.3 billion. He gave hundreds of millions to many organizations, including an estimated $141 million to the University of Michigan. When Taubman entered the boardroom, the level of deference shown by Fords, "auto" and "chemical" alike, bordered on obsequious. He would occasionally opine about something he knew little or nothing about, and all present would hang on his every oracle-like utterance. I report this to illustrate the phenomenon, not to demean the participants.

Invoking the post-Enron movie title, the wealthy men (and they are mostly men) behind education reform are convinced that they are "The Smartest Guys in the Room." Because things worked for them, they honestly believe they know how things work, or should work, in every other realm. Move the levers, let free markets yield optimal outcomes, develop models, define benchmarks, utilize the right metrics, and make efficient use of capital. The recalcitrant, lethargic, failing education system will eventually respond, because that is the way their world works.

The problem is that education and schools are not upscale shopping malls (Taubman), chemicals (Ford), automobiles (Ford), computer operating systems (Gates), insurance and finance (Broad), or retail behemoths with no conscience (Walton). Education and schools are about children – real, living, breathing, complicated, tender, diverse children. There is no model, no assembly line, and no template or standard methodology that can serve them well.

This is a very important historical perspective and explains why the factory model of education is prevailing in the 21st century. In short, business leaders and free market economic principles have gained increasing control over education. Education has become highly dependent on philanthropy, as public funding has declined. Philanthropists didn't make their fortunes as violinists, so they bring their business perspectives to bear on the institutions they support. As the old saying goes, "If your only tool is a hammer, every problem is a nail." Today's economist-driven version of education reform is the hammer that mistakes America's children, particularly the poorest kids of color, as nails to pound.

Consider the existential threats that inspired this book, particularly the threats of nuclear winter and of irreversible climate change. Many of the architects of education policy directly benefit from the activities that exacerbate these threats. The Koch brothers and Walton family members are not funding education reform because they think the world needs less carbon emissions or fewer material goods. It seems fair to assert that they are more interested in training compliant workers for their fossil fuel and resource-depleting businesses than in raising thinkers and revolutionaries, who will better equipped to deal with the existential risks posed by the inevitable severe, possibly catastrophic, climate and environmental changes that continued use of fossil fuels and exploitation of natural resources will bring about.

Politics and conspiracy theories (as education reformers love to dismiss concerns over privatization) aside, there is a heartbreaking aspect of contemporary conventional education policy that is seldom discussed. All of the language of education reform is barren and pragmatic. There is little mention of kindness, diversity or vulnerability. Schools and children seem to matter only to the extent that improvements in education will enhance America's place in the global economy. "Kids must have the skills to compete with the Chinese." "We need to invest in STEM programs to prepare students for the 21st century economy." Ask an unemployed Ph.D. engineer or mathematician about the mythological glut of unfilled, high paying jobs! A 2013 article in *The Atlantic* titled "The Ph.D. Bust: America's Awful Market for Young Scientists – in 7 Charts", thoroughly debunks that part of the STEM myth. [18]

All this rhetoric is about utility, never about joy or fulfillment. Particularly in schools that serve the poorest children, the curriculum is narrow and the discipline is severe. Poor kids are seen as problems to solve, not as children to love.

Is it really only children of privilege who can aspire to be poets and artists? The programs designed for poor children demand a high level of compliance and conformity. When you read the descriptions of charter schools like those whose policies I quote verbatim in Chapter 8, can you believe that educational reformers want these children to be truly free to grow and develop into whatever gorgeous wildflower was their destiny or dream, to be the skeptics our world so desperately needs, or iconoclasts who see what others don't?

This disparity in how we treat children is symptomatic of a larger social problem. For example, when privileged folk sow their wild seeds in adolescence, it makes for amusing stories and a bit of street credibility. When young black men and women sow a few seeds in adolescence, it makes for a stint in jail and low or no employment for a lifetime. Politicians like Mike Huckabee chastise black musicians for violent or sexually charged lyrics while jamming with the despicable, misogynist Ted Nugent.

We are drowning in this kind of double standard. As will be a frequent echo in these pages, the approaches to education for poor children of color are tainted with subconscious racism. Not bigotry. Not hatred. Just an unspoken assumption that these kids need to be in "no excuses" schools, suggesting that their disadvantages are an "excuse" to use, not an injustice to address.

The constricting environments created by education reform do damage to kids that we seldom hear about. The propaganda of National School Choice Week and puff pieces about "no excuses" charter schools get widespread media attention. Young women and men like Jamal (not his real name, but a very real story) get very little attention.

Jamal attended a Democracy Prep charter school a few years back during the time a current Calhoun teacher taught there. Jamal is a young man of color with a single parent mother. Her intentions were good but her resources were sparse. They were homeless from time to time. Jamal went to Democracy Prep with the hope that it would give him a better chance in life.

Jamal was not – is not – inclined toward unquestioning compliance. By his own report, corroborated by his teacher, Jamal respectfully, but assertively, questioned authority. When his questions drew "consequences," he had the unmitigated gall to ask, "Why?" This invariably drew the next consequence about which he would ask, "But why? What did I do?" No matter the triviality of the original infraction, it was the questions that quickly led to yellow shirt and shunning. Democracy Prep claims to have given Jamal chances that he "blew," but he eventually became a statistic – one of many ejected from the school because of a failure to adequately comply and conform. I have read scores of similar stories from parents who are outraged that the promise of an uplifting experience crashed into the hard ground of "no excuses" reform. In Chapter 8, I offer, verbatim, the disciplinary policy of Democracy Prep at the time Jamal was enrolled.

Jamal's teacher had foregone a high paying position in a private school to teach at several charter schools, including Democracy Prep. He is a man of deep convictions, great empathy and a strong social conscience. He wanted to do meaningful work. Jamal's experience and others like it were profoundly disappointing to him. A good, good man with many years of experience and extraordinary teaching skills was not what "no-excuses" charter schools wanted. One of the charter movement's leading lights confirmed this by telling him, "You are a creative teacher and creative teachers cannot work here." Just what kind of "democracy" is Democracy Prep preparing children for?

With the teacher's support, Jamal came to Calhoun. I wish I could report a heartwarming success story. He did not graduate, although our relationship with him continues. I know him well. He is smart, courageous, a young father, a gifted musician and a highly principled man. It is incomprehensible that any school would have found his pride a reason to label him a miscreant. For what these schools do to boys and girls like Jamal there is indeed "no excuse."

This face of education reform is largely hidden from view.

Are the parents of poor children of color not entitled to the same hopes and dreams as their more privileged peers? Might these children lead satisfying lives too or should they just be trained to be useful?

But that's a false choice. There is no dilemma. There is no tension between a satisfying life and a useful life. They arise from the same humane, loving, progressive practices. Passion, curiosity, eccentricity, originality, humor and empathy make for a rich and full life. These qualities are also what make the best leaders, artists, entrepreneurs, lovers, friends – and employees.

Flawed Assessments of Schools

This may be the most counterintuitive issue in educational debate. A nearly universal misunderstanding of "good schools" inhibits a rational analysis of children and learning. I emphasize this issue because the embrace of conventional education, and the uninformed disregard for progressive education, is perpetuated by this distortion.

This is particularly true in the case of charter schools, where an extreme form of conventional pedagogy and discipline is falsely claimed to have resulted in improved achievement. I hope to make a convincing case that this "success" is contrived and that it would be relatively meaningless even if true.

The criteria by which we deem schools "good" or "bad" are commonly held in our culture. Perhaps understandably, schools are judged by the success, or lack of success, of their students or graduates. Success is judged by grades, test scores and the next step taken in educational sequence, whether in higher education, secondary education, or primary education. This is true whether schools are public, private or charter. This universal belief distorts nearly every aspect of education policy and practice.

The most obvious example of this phenomenon is rankings

of America's colleges and universities, like those in the *U.S News and World Report*. Each year millions of copies fly off the shelves before the ink is dry as students, parents, college counselors and university PR departments check to see who's on top or moving up. Schools are divided into tiers. Being relegated to the 2nd tier from the 1st or to the 3rd from the 2nd is an institutional tragedy. As the rankings shift, the applicant pool shifts with it. In this annual farce, as the applicant pool shifts, the rankings shift too. As any educator knows, among the criteria used to rank colleges are the number of applicants (more is good) and the number of acceptances (less is good). Therefore a primary way to improve your ranking is to entice far more applicants than necessary and shatter as many young dreams as possible by rejecting them.

Of course that's not the only criterion. You also have to do well in a popularity poll with other educators. Peer school administrators weigh in on each other's schools. It is a bit like the homecoming queen and her court casting ballots for each other. College counselors at high schools also have a say. Here too, it is primarily a popularity contest. Who would think Harvard anything but top tier? These ratings require no actual familiarity with the school or what happens in its classrooms. It's all about reputation.

And, of course, there are the test scores. There are always the test scores. The median and mean SAT and ACT scores of incoming freshmen play a significant part in the rankings, as do their grade point averages. So, de facto, a school is "good" because the students they accept gamed the system brilliantly, often by way of thousands of dollars of SAT prep and as many AP courses as could be crammed into their schedules.

Alumni giving and faculty compensation are criteria too. These things are all connected, as the richest schools have the best reputations, which attract the most alumni support, which builds the largest endowments, which fuel the higher salaries, which improve the rankings, which burnishes the reputations, which attracts more applicants, which allows the college to turn away more kids – and on it goes in a merry circle.

Where in this public relations exercise does one find the actual quality of the learning experience? Defenders of this elitist game claim, with some very slight justification, that collecting a bunch of high-octane achievers enhances the educational environment. But, as I address later in Chapter 5, the process is more likely to enhance the population of the school's mental health department and the eating disorder ward in the local hospital.

This does not mean that the "winners" provide a lousy education. Schools with sterling reputations may be wonderful, at least in some ways, but the rankings and the criteria in the rankings have almost nothing to do with educational quality. Some of the institutions ranked at the top are notorious for large undergraduate lecture classes, and for the use of graduate assistants acting as surrogates for the famous professors who teach graduate students and appear on cable television. By contrast, some lower tier colleges have brilliant faculty members, small, engaging classes, and powerful student/faculty relationships that inspire and motivate.

A different version of the same game permeates private school education in America, particularly in major cities and elite boarding schools. High schools select students who are most likely to perpetuate their reputation by gaining admission to top tier colleges. Middle schools pick kids who are most likely to get into the high schools that predict matriculation at Ivy League schools. All the way down to nursery school, parents and schools are co-conspirators in this crazy chase. It is a process of selection, self-selection, pretense and stress. It has nothing to do with children or learning.

I have fun each year poking at this ridiculous, anxiety-provoking private school culture during the admission process.

"If you want to win the game you have to start early," I suggest. "Tutoring for a pre-school admission test is a small price for your 18 month-old to pay for an eventual ticket to Princeton." And, wishing to be helpful, "Here at Calhoun we offer really early admission for truly ambitious families. For this Pre-natal Admission Program (PAP) we accept amniocentesis reports or ultra-sound images. For latecomers, we will grudgingly accept APGAR scores, if it's all you have."

In a speech several years ago I described a hypothetical, analogous school process. What if the goal of families and schools was to have really fast runners? (This is not so very far from reality.) Have 100 kids line up and race for 10 spots. Admit the winners. Do that every year. Then, when a particular child gains a few pounds in puberty or turns out to be one of those kids who develop quickly and then taper off, counsel her out saying condescendingly, "School X might be a better fit for you." Have a new set of kids line up to race for the newly vacant spot. At the end of this charade, pat yourself on the back for having the fastest graduates in town.

Once again, this doesn't mean that such schools are bad schools. It only means that such schools are not good schools merely by virtue of selecting kids who are most likely to do well in the ways they value. Regardless of the quality of teaching and learning in such a school, the culture created through this wild chase can do a great deal of harm, both cognitively and emotionally.

But the privileged worlds of higher education and private schools are not major factors driving policy and practice in American schools. The mistaken beliefs about "good" and "bad" public schools are much more damaging.

In the '60s I graduated from one of America's top-ranked public high schools. Among its great assets was the school orchestra, considered among the nation's finest secondary school ensembles. The truth is that the school had very little to do with the fine orchestra. I can't recall a single accomplished orchestra member who learned to play an instrument primarily at school. Most of the advanced violinists, including me, studied with the same teacher at the Cleveland Institute of Music. Many of the school orchestra members came from musical families and frequently attended Cleveland Orchestra concerts. The assumption was that the school had a superb music program. I can't recall anything good about it at all, other than that there were many kids who could already play well.

Such was also the case with the school's academic program, which had many National Merit Scholars and a fine college placement record. The assumption was that the school had a superb faculty and curriculum, but I can't recall any particularly powerful educational experiences. This school's students were capable in conventional ways and came from relatively privileged families. The community was convinced that it had great schools. In reality, the schools had a great community. Within the conventional construct, the school was fine and I genuinely enjoyed some of the teachers and classes. But I don't believe the school or its teachers were necessarily "better" than the inner city schools just a mile or two away, where poverty and racism flourished.

The extent of this misunderstanding is remarkable. In the early summer of 2016 I had a serendipitous meeting with a leader of a progressive school who had previously worked in Cleveland. When learning that I grew up in Cleveland, she asked, "Did you go to one of the independent schools or one of the excellent public schools in the suburbs?" It was an innocent question, but revealed her automatic assessment of a school based on its privileged community, rather than on anything about the school itself.

My intent is not to disparage either the school or the community, it is to point out that the frenzy over school reform is a reverse analog of my childhood experience. Politicians, reformers and pundits claim that we have a great nation with lousy schools. What we have are the same schools we always had, with a deteriorating national community.

School reputations, like that of my high school, are primarily the artifact of privilege – the greater the privilege, the better the reputation of the schools in the neighborhood – the deeper the poverty, the worse the school's reputation. This demographic sorting is nothing new. It's just worse now. And reputation plays an ongoing role in deepening the chasm of inequity. Folks with capital and credit buy homes in neighborhoods with "good" schools. Real estate listings in communities of privilege almost always brag about the schools. This desirability factor drives up prices, thereby hastening America's re-segregation by race and class. Higher prices mean higher property values, which yield higher property taxes, which are still the primary funding mechanism for public schools. So not only do the schools have more resources, they have families in the community who are able to provide a variety of enriching experiences for their children.

As in Cleveland Heights, affluent towns all around America think they have great schools, when in fact the schools have privileged communities. Communities with resources have "good" schools, poor neighborhoods have "bad" schools, and folks think that's just the way it is. These things have been believed for generations.

But now, in the standards and accountability era, there is an additional way of differentiating the "good" schools from the "bad" – by testing their students and then ranking schools by those test scores. The unquestioned assumption is that higher test scores mean better schools. But this just isn't true either.

Public schools all over America are judged by the standardized test results of their students. In many, perhaps most, communities the test results are published in local newspapers or available online. The continued existence of a school often depends on its standardized test scores. Whether in public or quasi-public (charters and chains) schools, a version of the college ranking system or the private school chase for glory is now playing out. Neighborhood public schools are labeled "failing" on the basis of test scores and closed, often to be replaced by a charter operation that boasts of higher test scores.

Charter schools attract hundreds of millions of dollars in private support from foundations and hedge funds. They have to prove their mettle by flaunting their high test scores. This is big, big business. Many parents choose schools, when possible, based on test scores. Teachers are evaluated on the basis of test scores – with their jobs at stake. In Atlanta and other cities, administrators and teachers have been charged with crimes for manipulating test scores. Cheating scandals have erupted in many communities. When politicians and education bureaucrats talk about high stakes testing, they aren't kidding!

Constant testing hasn't made any school better. I liken it to assuming that Hansel and Gretel will gain weight just by being weighed more often. Schools have gotten steadily worse as a result of the emphasis on testing and test preparation.

What has occurred is a complex sorting mechanism. The schools, particularly the most highly praised charter schools, do several things to produce better scores. Some evidence, particularly as it pertains to the much-celebrated Success Academies in New York City, indicates that students are suspended and expelled at a much higher rate than at the ordinary public schools in their neighborhoods. Several studies show that charter schools enroll significantly fewer students with learning challenges or students whose first language is other than English. While some of the research is controversial, in the aggregate there appears to be a fair amount of what is termed "creaming." And, of course, there is ample evidence that charter school students have the benefit of parents who have sought out the charter school, thereby making the schools selective, at least on the basis of this one predictor of success.

Because the charter industry plays such a huge role in perpetuating what I've characterized as the mythology of "good schools," further documentation of the statements above is necessary.

Luis Huerta is an associate professor of education and

public policy at Teachers College, Columbia University and the co-editor of the journal, *Educational Evaluation and Policy Analysis*. In a December, 2014 article in *The New York Times* [19] he wrote:

> *High-suspension rates coupled with the fact that charter schools seldom enroll more students once others drop out, means that the test scores of many charters only reflect the achievement of the survivors who have endured a school's full treatment. What results are unreliable data that risk exposing the self-acclaimed "high performing charter school" status adopted by many charters, and reducing it to a myth.*

> *Policy makers should resist being seduced by achievement scores and, instead, hold charter schools accountable and aligned with the long-standing purpose of public schools.*

> *What's more, these high-suspension rates are fueled by strict "no excuses" disciplinary policies employed by many charter schools, especially those serving low-income minority students in urban areas. Over the last three years, charter schools in Washington suspended over 25 students for every 1 student suspended in regular public schools. Nine out of the 10 schools in Massachusetts with the highest suspension rates were charters. This type of data has prompted the U.S. Secretary of Education to sternly implore charters to address high-suspension rates. Yet there is no evidence indicating charter administrators have reacted.*

> *Of course, high-suspension rates may also be influenced by the perverse incentives promoted by market competition among charter school operators. Charter management*

organizations are competing for market share in urban neighborhoods through the branding and franchising of a schooling model that engages selectively in deciding which students they serve. This competitive environment, in some cases uninhibited by public accountability, may lead charters to promote their franchise, and lose site (sic) of the kids they are charged with serving. [20]

Carol Burris is principal at South Side High School in Rockville Centre, N.Y. and the author of *On the Same Track: How Schools Can Join the Twenty-First-Century Struggle against Resegregation.* In the December, 2014 article in *The New York Times* she wrote:

Charter schools often cherry-pick through attrition. When students leave because the schools are too demanding, the charters are not obligated to fill the empty seats. New York's Harlem Success 1 Academy had 127 first graders in 2009. When those students arrived in grade six last year, only 82 remained. As students moved through the grades, Success 1 lost over 35 percent of the cohort. In comparison, a nearby neighborhood school, P.S. 191 Amsterdam, saw its 2008-09 first grade cohort increase from 39 students to 55 by grade six. We who teach in open-enrollment public schools must take every student that moves in – regardless of their age, learning disability, the time of entrance or when they last attended school.

What accounts for the high attrition rates at charters? Their strict discipline codes and higher rates of suspension, retention and expulsion are well documented. In 2013, the SUNY Charter Institute, which authorizes charters, reported problems with disciplinary practices, including suspensions, at several Harlem Success Academies. When students are pushed out or leave their charter school, they enter the public schools discouraged and further behind. [21]

Richard Kahlenberg and Halley Potter are fellows at *The Century Foundation*. In the December, 2014 article in *The New York Times* they wrote:

Charter schools educate larger proportions of low-income and minority students than traditional public schools, but reports show that charter schools in cities like Boston, Chicago and Washington have much higher suspension and expulsion rates than regular public schools.

Without taking those statistics into account, some conservative public policy makers draw the wrong lessons from charter schools. They point to the impressive test scores of some high-profile charter schools with high poverty rates and no teacher unions to argue, for example, that the challenges of concentrated poverty can be systematically overcome in regular public schools if we just eliminate collective bargaining agreements for teachers.

They hold up the high test scores of some charter schools as a model, without acknowledging that these are the test scores of the students who are educated in drastically different peer environments than those found in traditional public schools. [22]

As is true with colleges and private schools, this method of identifying and retaining kids who are more likely to succeed does not mean that a school is "bad." Such schools could be quite wonderful – except they're not. They are beholden to funders and held hostage by test scores. Like public schools, charters have to prove and re-prove their efficacy by demonstrating ever-rising test scores. If not, their charters can be revoked or the gravy train can stall.

So across the entire spectrum of education in America there is a set of factors considered in determining which schools are *good*:

- *Good* if your applicants have very high scores on standardized tests before they ever set foot in your school. This is true for colleges, private schools, and selective public schools;

- *Good* if you are a college or private school, attract lots of applicants, and deny admission to most of them;

- *Good* if your students got really good grades in the school previously attended, before they ever set foot in your school;

- *Good* if your graduates (from nursery school, pre-school, kindergarten, middle school, high school) go to the next school in chronological sequence that sends the most kids to the most selective of the next schools in chronological sequence;

- *Good* public or charter school if your students have scored well on standardized tests, even if you have gamed the system as described above.

The further a school deviates from these criteria, the more its ranking or reputation suffers. These five criteria have nothing to do with the quality of the education provided by a school, and all five of these criteria drive bad educational practices in several or many ways.

This fundamental misunderstanding about what constitutes

a good school infects almost all discourse about education and education reform. Even the good guys fall for it. In an October 2014 piece in *Politico Magazine* titled "The Plot Against Public Education: How millionaires and billionaires are ruining our schools," [23] former New York Times columnist Bob Herbert makes a compelling case against the philanthropically driven reform movement.

Even the estimable Herbert inadvertently capitulates to the erroneous notion that test scores mean something important. He rightly notes that Bill Gates and other billionaires have done nothing to improve test scores or close the so-called achievement gap (largely a white/black disparity in test scores). By stipulating that test scores are the measure of a good school, he and nearly all other critics perpetuate the same poor practices in schools. Even well-intended critics of education reform merely point out that the reforms didn't raise test scores, not that test scores are the wrong objective.

Perhaps because it is the cultural currency for understanding achievement, test performance pops up in unlikely places. Howard Gardner, whose work I greatly admire, reverts to citing test scores when praising the outcomes in schools based on his own multiple intelligences theory. I wish he and others would avoid this justification, however tempting it may be. When we stipulate to the idea that success is accurately measured by test results, we become complicit in perpetuating bad education.

I offer the rather ironic argument that the classroom practices employed in the service of improving test scores will repress real intellectual development, perhaps guaranteeing that even successful test takers will do less well on future tests. Several years ago, NYC pundits and politicians seemed befuddled that 4th grade test scores had improved but that 8th grade test scores had dropped. I believe the daily "drill and kill" practices that temporary lifted 4th grade scores were at the root of poor performance thereafter.

Reputation and test scores are not a meaningful indicator of a school's effectiveness, but they are the common currency of success in our culture. Since progressive schools resist these measures, how do we know we are doing well by our students? In a progressive school, we measure our success by the arc of progress observed in each student, on his or her terms. When we issue lengthy narrative reports, we often hear parents exclaim, "You know our child better than we do!" We hear the passion in students' voices and we see the light in their eyes. We marvel at their originality and we applaud their courage. We watch their love of one another and their powerful sense of social justice. We see them go to the colleges and universities of their choice, and we take satisfaction as they assume leadership positions. We hear constant reports from colleges about their superior writing skills, their enthusiasm, their self-advocacy, and their humanity.

History offers only one large-scale, significant study of the efficacy of progressive education. In the 1930's, the Carnegie Corporation and the General Education Board funded the *Eight Year Study*, [24] comparing outcomes between a cohort of alternative schools that had adopted progressive practices and a similar sized group of conventional schools. The purpose of the study was to examine whether students who were not trained in conventional college preparatory programs could go to and succeed in college. As the title suggests, the study followed students from each cohort for a full eight years of high school and college. Students from the progressive schools demonstrated equal or superior outcomes in every dimension. Students from the most radically progressive schools had the most impressive long-term results.

This study explicitly demonstrated the superiority of a progressive approach. Now, advances in human understanding, primarily in psychology and neurobiology, give us the scientific reasons that progressive educators had it right all along.

Schools at the Barbell Ends

The consequences of repeatedly turning away from a progressive, and toward an increasingly rigid conventional model, reach across a broad continuum of race, class and geography in America. Those consequences are most severe at the barbell ends of society – in the most privileged and least privileged communities. Too many of our schools are harming children.

At each end of the privilege continuum, the weight has gotten significantly heavier in recent years. The pressure to achieve conspicuous success in privileged communities has wreaked havoc on kids' well-being. And the hard-driving, militaristic practices imposed on young, poor children, mostly of color, are punitive, condescending and ineffective.

I don't mean to create a false equivalence. The deleterious effects of pressure to achieve in privileged communities are not equivalent to the abandonment of poor communities of color. Those who enjoy privilege can cure the ills accompanying their privilege, but the desperate circumstances in poor communities require an urgent collective response and the investment of billions of dollars. Individual children are being harmed at each end of America's privilege continuum and I hope to give support to those who seek to mitigate this harm, wherever it falls.

Several years ago, at an admissions open house, I talked about the collateral damage of ultra-high achievement. Particularly in communities of privilege, the competitive pressure to get the brass ring of acceptance to a highly selective college has dramatically increased. This is especially pernicious among young women due to a phenomenon Stanford's Denise Pope has termed, "Doing School." [25]

At the open house I described the growing incidence of eating disorders, depression, binge drinking and other physical responses to chronic stress seen at the most elite institutions. There is a mountain of anecdotal evidence, including dozens of first hand testimonials I've received from faculty members at elite colleges, that too many students arrive at their coveted destinations suffering from severe "burn-out." In addition to the physical symptoms, they appear incurious, dispassionate and lost. As Jerome Bruner predicted, they are the end game of the way "learning" is internalized in an early, high-pressure academic environment. These students have been conditioned to do what I called "learning to the test." They have a primary, if not sole, goal of getting the answers right on the next exam and never soiling their impeccable resumes with any A-minuses.

This conditioning affects more than the academic realm. In a December 2014 piece in *The New York Times* about student activism [26] – or lack thereof – Richard Parker, a Harvard lecturer on public policy and a veteran 1960s activist, observed that students today are more cautious and career-oriented. "There is diversity on the input side, and standardization on the output side," Parker said. "If you give the students a clear structure, they function well. Give them a range of autonomy, they're more tentative."

As an example, I cite a lovely chat with a recent Calhoun graduate who went on to Princeton. I should note that she did so without undue stress, without any class ranking, without any AP or honors courses, very few exams and with minimal school or family pressure. She remarked, as have many of our graduates regardless of their college choice, that many of her freshmen peers were burned out and incurious, despite – or perhaps because of – all the achievement. But the funniest part of her report was about an essay assignment.

The professor said, "Write about whatever you'd like. I just want to get a sense of your thinking and your writing skills."

"But, but …" replied several students, "What do you want us to write about?"

"Whatever interests you," replied the professor.

"But what are we supposed to write about? What are we supposed to be interested in?"

The exchange consumed several minutes, clearly frustrating the professor and amusing my young friend. How can these bright students change the world if they don't even know what they are "interested in?"

Back to the admissions event. At the end of my speech, a parent of a prospective 9th grader approached me. He introduced himself as an administrator, involved in admissions, at an Ivy League professional school. Responding to this part of my speech he said, "About 50% of the students in our current first year class are in mental health treatment." Even with my sensitivity to this issue, I was astonished.

In the fall of 2014 I had verification of this collateral damage. I hosted a breakfast with parents of pre-school or kindergarten children who were new to the school. In the context of talking about why they chose a progressive school and how it was going for them, this issue of stress and pressure arose. It was clear that part of their attraction to Calhoun was the relative lack of competitive pressure and stress. To emphasize the point, I related the story of the Ivy League administrator (whose son indeed came to Calhoun) and his report of 50% of first year students in mental health treatment.

I knew that two of the new parents in the room teach undergraduates at Columbia University. I anticipated that they might balk at this statistic, become defensive, or report a much different experience. Both of them responded, "I think that percentage is probably low."

Denise Pope's book is titled, *"Doing School" How We Are Creating a Generation of Stressed Out, Materialistic and Miseducated Students* [25]. Therein she explicates, in research-supported detail, the factors that create the culture of achievement to which I refer. The book follows the tortuous path to the brass ring followed by five students, all from the same "good" suburban school, but each from a very different background. From Pope's first chapter:

> *These students explain that they are busy at what they call "doing school." They realized that they are caught in a system where achievement depends more on "doing" – going through the correct motions – than on learning and engaging with the curriculum. Instead of thinking deeply about the content of their courses and delving into projects and assignments, the students focus on managing*

the workload and honing strategies that will help them achieve high grades. They learn to raise their hands even when they don't know the answers to the teacher's questions in order to appear interested. They understand the importance of forming alliances and classroom treaties to win favors from teachers and administrators. Some feel compelled to cheat and to contest certain grades and decisions in order to get the scores they believe they need for the future. As Kevin (one of the students she follows) asserts:

"People don't go to school to learn. They go to get good grades which brings them to college, which brings them to the high-paying job, which brings them to happiness, so they think. But basically, grades is where it's at."

Kevin provides a pretty clear example of the inevitable results of a system of extrinsic motivation. Basically, in America's conventional schools, "grades is where it's at."

It is not only "grades is where it's at" that creates the pathology at this end of the American barbell. Other negative things come along with the extrinsically driven system. Once caught in the maw of high achievement culture, students are expected to do long, long hours of homework. Even if a school does not explicitly require 5-7 hours of homework per night, the requirement is implicit in the quest for perfection.

This implicit demand has the related effect of sleep deprivation. The Mayo Clinic reports that teenagers need about 9 hours of sleep per night. Most teens, particularly in the "doing school" cohort, are seriously sleep deprived. Sleep deprivation impairs cognitive function. Talk about an idiotic educational practice – create a climate of uber-achievement that depends on doing so much homework that it erodes cognitive function! Sleep deprivation can also lead to depression, anxiety, type-2 diabetes, high blood pressure and impaired judgment. This is what thousands of schools are complicit in perpetuating – but we want our children to succeed. Their health is evidently a small price to pay.

This is one way we are the keeping up with South Koreans! A 2012 study of South Korean adolescents [27] revealed that they averaged 4.9 hours of sleep in the service of their culture's emphasis on academic success. This would be somewhat barbaric, even if it were necessary. But it's not.

Two books published in 2006 fully rebut any such notion. *The Case Against Homework* [28], by Sara Bennett and Nancy Kalish, provides a very thorough review of the ways in which long hours of homework harm rather than help young folks. Bennett and Kalish were inspired by their own children's misery and decided to do something about it. Lots of homework is not only unnecessary, but it prevents kids from spending time doing things of much greater value. Alfie Kohn's *The Homework Myth* [29] makes similarly compelling arguments from a philosophical, psychological and neurobiological perspective.

All of the evidence suggests that homework has rapidly diminishing returns beyond an hour or two per night, even in high school. Despite these highly publicized books, book tours, school presentations, conferences and a growing pile of research, barely a dent has been made in the daily practices at most schools.

This evidence eludes or frustrates many parents, educators and students who, despite the research, continue to believe that stress and competition are necessary means to an important end. Countless times, when I conclude a pleasant diatribe on this topic, a parent or visitor will say something like, "Well, that's what my education was like and I guess I turned out alright!"

Those who have endured a stressful, elite education are inferring a cause and effect relationship that doesn't exist, at least not in the way they assume. Their success is the consequence of a system that privileges the IQ-style of intelligence that Howard Gardner rejects as too limited and limiting. Their success is likely to have been, in part, a result of experiences they enjoyed before school age, after school hours, and despite their teachers and curriculum. They are likely to have been members of highly verbal families, scored well on linguistic/logical-mathematical assessments, enjoyed trips to museums, had private music lessons and so on.

This is an individual manifestation of precisely what I described when discussing how we evaluate schools. It is an education version of the "born on third base and thinking he hit a triple" phenomenon that has been used to characterize certain political leaders. There are, of course, many exceptions to this generalization, but the exceptions don't disprove the rule.

This analysis of privileged schools is not intended to indict or vilify those who attended such schools. And I surely don't mean to criticize those among my colleagues who preside over schools with some of these characteristics. I hope many of them will agree with much of what I've written. I know one colleague did.

Some years ago I wrote a letter to the New York Times, briefly summarizing the self-fulfilling game of selection, ranking and sorting. I argued, within the NYT's 150-word limit, that college placement statistics don't reflect anything about the quality of a school. I wondered – worried a little – that friends who led schools with glittery placement statistics would be offended. My phone rang. It was Henry (Hank) Moses, the Head of Trinity School in Manhattan, a school that certainly fits the "glittery" description. I knew Hank fairly well and liked him very much. He tragically died, much too young, not many years later. Hank started, "I'm really pissed." "Oops," I said. "Didn't mean to piss you off." "Well you did. I'm pissed that you didn't ask me to co-sign the letter."

Many fine educators push back against this culture of stress and empty achievement every day, in Manhattan and across the country. Whether they identify as "progressive" or not, they know as much as or more than I do. If anything, I hope this book can be a support in their work to bring more sanity to their privileged institutions.

This disclaimer must also explain why so many graduates of highly competitive, privileged schools are quite brilliant, creative, imaginative and ethical. It's not only because they "won" the game in a system that values their attributes. Most privileged schools actually do a great deal of progressive educating. In small classes students are doing projects, debating important questions, choosing to investigate things of great interest and being exposed to the arts in abundance. Private education is also enlivened by this counter-intuitive reality – independent schools have become much more diverse as our nation's public schools have been increasingly re-segregated. This dimension of private education adds great richness and is an achievement of real note in the independent school world. The excessive competition and stress in a school's culture may have other, negative, consequences, but the education itself is often terrific.

Privileged schools are also immune, in whole or in part, from the misguided public policies that drive bad education. Private schools (more euphemistically called independent schools in order to dodge the appearance of elitism) are not required to adhere to public mandates for testing and accountability. But even in the public sector, privilege lends power. The anti-testing movement emerged initially in more affluent neighborhoods and communities, and is thankfully now more widespread. Scarsdale, for example, a wealthy town in Westchester County, NY, was among the first systems to say, "We're not going to do it."

Less-privileged schools are not so lucky. Some years ago, in the relative calm before the current storm of education reform, charters, vouchers, and ham-handed accountability, I was invited to be on an education panel at a Harlem community board meeting. I was the only private school person present and I attended with some reluctance. Not that I felt I would be poorly treated. Quite to the contrary, and as I expected, I received a warm welcome. My reluctance was that I didn't wish to be perceived as "the expert" who came from the more privileged part of the Upper Westside of Manhattan. The other panel members were teachers, administrators, parents and local politicians. I was also the only white person on the panel, which added to my inclination to be very deferential. But I had to talk. When my turn came, I said something like this:

I have no standing to suggest what you should do about your neighborhood schools, other than lobby for more money, fewer tests, and smaller classes. I'm head of a progressive private school on 81st Street. We believe that effective education is very difficult when class size exceeds 15 (audible gasp). It's not because we have so much money that it doesn't matter. We are not one of the really wealthy schools. It's just that we know that understanding every student, hearing each voice and organizing powerful experiences, gets significantly more difficult in classes beyond 15. And we start off with students who are most likely to succeed, whose parents earn a fair (or excessive!) income and who had pre-school or other really important early childhood experiences.

We don't have magical solutions. You could take our faculty members, as wonderful as they are, our curriculum, as imaginative as it is, and plunk it all down in one of your neighborhood schools and I doubt it would make any significant difference. It's clear to me that you have wonderful teachers. But if the most privileged kids, who are picked because they are the most likely to succeed, need classes of 15 or fewer, then maybe children who have much less privilege might need classes of 8 in order to get the same understanding, attention and opportunity to find their "voices." That costs money. When our city – our country – makes that kind of financial commitment to education, perhaps things will change. Until then it's all talk.

That was more than a dozen years ago and the "all talk" has continued unabated. In fact, things have gotten worse. The tenacity of the problem is rooted in the same misunderstanding of education that accompanied each juncture I've described:

- When progressive education "lost" to factory education around one hundred years ago;

- When *A Nation at Risk* put the nation at greater risk by doubling down on the industrial model;

- When Gardner was not heeded in the early 1990's and IQ-style education prevailed;

- And now, as we leave children to slide down the slope, as well-funded politicians and their corporate benefactors Race to the Top.

The current dominance of the industrial, uniform approach to learning is especially damaging in urban schools, public and charter.

Putting "public" and "charter" in the same basket is misleading. In major urban areas like New York City, Detroit, New Orleans, Chicago, Los Angeles, Philadelphia, Atlanta, there is a stark division between regular public schools and charter schools. Charter schools are "public" only in that they get public funding. They systematically evade public oversight and accountability.

Most teachers and administrators in non-charter public schools are resistant to increased pressure and testing. I've talked with hundreds of public school teachers and leaders who are terribly frustrated. They know better, but are hamstrung by the demands of public policy. Kids, schools and teachers are all under the gun to produce better test scores. They would rather not work this way, but they have no choice. Educational reformers blame this resistance on intransigent, self-protective teacher unions and incompetent teachers, but there is no evidence to support those assertions. Teachers and their unions are no better or worse than decades ago. Teachers toe the line out of necessity, teach to the test for survival, and push back against the toxic tide of reform to the extent possible.

In addition to dealing with testing and accountability pressure, public schools are drastically underfunded and under-equipped. Most schools are dependent on property tax revenues, and real estate values have declined in many communities. While the financial implications are complicated, the rise of charter schools has put additional pressure on regular public schools. Students take public school funding with them when they leave their district school to attend a charter school.

The chickens of this fiscal undermining are coming home to roost. In Michigan – Detroit most particularly – public education is essentially dead. [30] Charter operators control some 80% of schools and are sucking the thin lifeblood out of already fragile communities. [31] The movement to expand charters is relentless with many states seeking to raise existing caps.

By contrast, charter schools embrace the industrial model with aggressive zeal. Everything is standardized. Teachers are scripted and learn tricks to manage classrooms. Slogans, signage, uniforms, hand gestures, call-and-response cheers and other things encourage – or even demand – conformity. The assumption behind the methodology is that a tightly controlled system can produce results. Tweak it here, adjust it there, run the kids through it, and outcomes can be measured. It is not coincidental that many education reformers are economists, not educators.

These hyper-conventional schools also disproportionally rely on young, poorly prepared teachers, particularly Teach for America graduates. Charter schools have very high faculty attrition rates, making relationships with students tenuous and short-term. I suspect that most charter school operators don't really care. Given the highly structured nature of many charter schools, the program can be implemented by almost any teacher willing to follow the script and work long hours. To stretch the industrial analogy, a teacher in this kind of system is like a worker on an assembly line. The parts, the order of assembly and the rate at which the line moves are all fixed. Parts and people are easily replaced.

Another disclaimer is necessary here. I truly admire the young teachers who are drawn to this work, often by a genuine desire to make a difference in children's lives. The fact that I find the educational philosophy wanting is not an explicit or implicit criticism of these teachers. Although confined by the system in which they work, many of them are loving, sensitive folks who care deeply about the children in their schools.

I've argued all of this before, in blog posts and newspaper columns, and incurred the wrath of many education reformers. In one such instance, the education reformer was one among many investment bankers who serve on the boards of charters and charter organizations. The financial industry, along with philanthropists including Bill and Melinda Gates, Eli Broad, the Walton family and others, are the prime movers behind this system. This particular charter leader was also a parent at Calhoun. Odd contrast that! One of my blog posts caught his attention and he met with me to, in his view, straighten out my misperceptions. We had a friendly conversation, during which I agreed to visit a charter school so that I might have first-hand experience rather than, as he saw it, crafting screeds from the comfort of my office.

I spent half a day at Harlem Success, the flagship school of Eva Moskowitz's considerable and growing New York City charter franchise. Part of my visit was an hour-long conversation with Moskowitz. She was pleasant and unpretentious – qualities not usually associated with her public image. I also found that she knew quite a bit about education.

The environment was not completely joyless. It was colorful and clean. But as I observed classes and kids, the conformity seemed stifling. Kids in groups, sitting on the floor in perfect circles in their neat uniforms, were attentively watching their teachers, who frequently commanded them to keep "eyes on the teacher." The students were not silent, but responses all came from very specific prompts requiring very specific answers. The teachers seemed to be following a very formal protocol. There were color-coded behavior charts on every classroom wall, where a child's ability to behave (or not) was publicly displayed. A level of privilege, or withholding of privilege, was associated with the color of a child's chart dots.

The New York Times published a video of a student being denigrated by a teacher in early 2016, inciting a flurry of criticism of Success Academies' harsh discipline. But, as with most other exposures of these practices, the furor was quickly extinguished by a flood of well-orchestrated propaganda and denial.

These kinds of charter schools are a junior size version of what I encountered in U.S. Army Officer Candidate School in 1967. Uniforms, walking silently in lines, judgment by test score, slogans on banners, catchy phrases to be repeated – all of these things extinguish individuality and reward unquestioning compliance. Education reform wants children to be good little soldiers.

Harlem Success, KIPP, Democracy Prep and other charter schools also feel children should pull mighty hard on their bootstraps. School hours are longer, Saturday classes are frequent expectations and school years are longer. Given the widely reported attrition rates, these schools' slogan might be, "Comply or Goodbye!"

I don't mean to unconditionally defend public schools and vilify charters. The charter movement, long before corporatization and standardization, arose because much of urban public education needed a good kick in the behind. There are remarkable charter schools rising from neighborhoods by parent initiative or founded by real visionaries. Many of these schools are quite progressive. But that initial impetus has been co-opted by charter chains and educational management organizations. These charter schools are the starkest examples of an industrial, standardized approach to education.

America has largely abandoned urban neighborhoods of color and these young children are paying the price for our neglect, either languishing in decaying, bleak public schools, or being trained in charter schools that resemble military academies.

The negative consequences of these approaches to education don't affect only children in the most and least privileged communities and schools. The policies and practices I've summarized have affected all schools, public and private, across America.

The majority of Americans attends, or attended, schools that are far from the barbell ends of privilege, ordinary schools in middle or working class communities – rural, suburban or urban. These schools, whether in Dallas or Des Moines, have been virtually indistinguishable throughout my lifetime. They all used the same or similar textbooks, the same or similar curricula and teaching. Some kids worked hard, got good grades and went to highly selective colleges. Many others muddled through, did well enough to go to a state school, community college or trade school. Others went from high school to work, in a local manufacturing facility or other business. Some joined the military or apprenticed in a trade. During my years in Ohio, Michigan, Vermont and New York, no one thought twice about any of this. It was just how things worked. I suspect this is still the case in many places around the nation.

I don't write with nostalgic intent. The conventional education provided in such schools wasn't ever particularly good. Some kids navigate this tedium more successfully than others, making schools sifters, where certain kinds of intelligence and temperament are rewarded and other kids are just not considered "college material." That unenlightened understanding of education has been the default approach for generations, and it has shortchanged a great many kids who are intelligent in different ways or don't succumb easily to dreary school routines. But that's nothing new.

The more recent intense focus on the most and least privileged schools and kids has negative consequences on education for all kids, not just those at the barbell ends.

The frantic chase for academic prestige, which produced Denise Pope's "Doing School" phenomenon and other toxic fumes in the most privileged schools, has polluted schools everywhere. In typical high schools, like those described above, the currency of "success" now includes the Advanced Placement curriculum, an increasing emphasis on GPA, and a competitive culture that drives more and more homework.

It wasn't long ago that only a few kids in places like rural Michigan ever gave a thought to Harvard, Yale or Princeton. Now, with US News Report rankings and other cultural pressure to achieve at the highest levels, millions more kids are in the rat race. This is a major cause of the dramatically increased numbers of applicants at the most selective colleges and universities.

It leads to the misperception that college admission is a rare prize, and that stress, competition, AP courses and perfect grades are the only avenue to success. But that is just not true. As has been widely documented, there is no shortage of places for students who aspire to college. An article in *The Atlantic* in April 2014 [32] reported that the number of college slots has increased and that the number of high school seniors is shrinking (slightly and temporarily). The prestige game is driving millions more American kids into thinking they've failed if they haven't gotten into a highly selective school. On balance it is no harder to get into a good college now than it was in 1992. It is just a whole lot harder to get into the most selective colleges, and these colleges have been complicit in making a whole lot of kids work a whole lot harder for a goal that is neither important nor attainable.

The collateral damage from the chase for glory in privileged communities is bad, but the political hand wringing over low achievement in poor urban schools has wreaked far more havoc. The concern over a small number of so-called failing schools has unleashed a torrent of really bad policy and practice that is washing over schools everywhere. Education reform is like trying to put out a fire in the closet by turning the hoses on the whole darned house. Which would be bad enough, but education reform policies are pouring gasoline, not water, on the fire.

My daughter is a wonderful teacher, trained in the Steiner (Waldorf) philosophy. For more than a dozen years she worked in several progressive Waldorf schools, engaging children in play-based activities, rich in the arts and lively, creative experiences, and all the other things a good progressive education provides. Then, in fall of 2014, she began work at a semi-rural public school in the Northeast Kingdom of Vermont. There, she encountered the slightly diluted, but still pointless, expectations of educational reform. I recently had a conversation with her in which she described, with real frustration, the automated assessment system the State of Vermont imposed on her pre-school. Several times a year she has to assess each of her students on 52 separate variables that supposedly represent important academic benchmarks for 4 year-old children.

Because real 4 year-olds are all over the developmental map, these benchmarks are meaningless, but she nonetheless must go through the exercise. And here's the real kicker – even the kindergarten teachers to whom the kids will be entrusted next do not review the assessments. The assessments are dumped into a massive database, never to be seen again. The hours wasted on this exercise are hours taken from real engagement with the kids, or from my daughter's time with her own child! She teaches pre-school, so the impact is less severe than on teachers of older kids. At least her job and school funding are not dependent on producing higher "letter recognition scores." The superintendent and principal clearly hired her because of her more progressive sensibilities. But she and they must work around the requirements of federal and state policy in order to do the work they love.

The expectations and requirements emanating from No Child Left Behind, Race to the Top, the Common Core and Every Child Succeeds Act are making life more difficult for teachers all around America – for absolutely no reason. Their schools are not failing, their students are doing no worse (or better) than they've ever done before, their communities aren't concerned about the schools, and yet the tentacles of mindless "reform" are strangling the life out of their schools.

The 2012 *MetLife Survey of The American Teacher: Challenges for School Leadership* report [33] shows that teacher morale is plummeting. In 2008, 62% of teachers reported being "satisfied" with their work. In 2012 that percentage shrank to 39%. This tragic fact is due to the policies and practices of educational reform and to the decreasing resources available to teachers. The extrinsic structures imposed on all public schools are the root cause of this demoralization. It is hard to imagine a scheme more dependent on extrinsic rewards and punishments than what is currently imposed on teachers.

Consider the intrinsic motivations that might lead a young woman or man into the teaching profession:

- A desire to instill a love in learning in children;

- Enjoying genuine, warm relationships with children;

- A deep interest in a particular subject and a desire to impart that passion to students;

- Wanting to help mold thoughtful, ethical citizens;

- Learning things along with the students;

- Helping each student to grow and thrive;

- Enjoyment of being part of a profession where practitioners share values and sense of purpose.

I'm sure every teacher could add to this list.

Now consider the extrinsic factors embedded in current

educational reform policies:

- Preparing students to perform well on standardized tests;

- Compensation that is contingent on students' test performance;

- Covering material that is provided, in most instances, by a third party;

- Expecting all students to attend to and master the same material and skills, regardless of their own interests and abilities;

- Doing these things as a condition of continued employment;

- Enforcing disciplinary procedures that degrade the student/ teacher relationship.

I'm sure every teacher could add to this list too.

As extrinsic rewards and punishments have become public policy, teachers' intrinsic motivation is declining proportionally. Add to that the gratuitous teacher bashing that is part of the anti-union, anti-tenure, pro-charter movement and the result is driving many of the finest teachers in America out of the profession. Teaching requires sacrifice enough, without having the personal satisfactions taken away too.

The teachers most affected by this shift from intrinsic to extrinsic are those in charters and other public schools that increasingly employ young men and women, like Teach for America (TFA) graduates, who have been told that these extrinsic motivators are necessary and good for children – and for them as well. Many quickly realize that this is a false promise. The burnout rate for these young teachers is frightening. According to a January 2014 report [34] by the National Education Policy Center at the School of Education, University of Colorado, Boulder, more than 50% of TFA graduates quit after 2 years and more than 80% leave after 3 years. I believe this is largely due to the policies and practices that have imposed extrinsic rewards and punishments on them while inhibiting those things which are intrinsically motivating to good teachers.

This epidemic of plummeting morale is not confined to young TFA graduates. In the Washington, D.C. system, plagued by serial scandals, 70% of teachers leave by the 5th year. Education reform has made the profession an untenable life choice for many teachers.

The annual attrition rate for faculty at Calhoun, where progressive practices keep intrinsic motivation alive, is less than 4%. And virtually none of those leaving are leaving the profession. They leave for various reasons, but they usually continue to teach. Teacher satisfaction needn't thrive only in explicitly progressive schools. Teachers in very conventional schools once had the autonomy to do many things that were essentially progressive – things like field trips, fun projects, musical theater, science experiments, debate classes, and other experiential, sensory-rich activities. Now, with the stringent, all-consuming expectations imposed by NCLB, RTTP and Common Core, good teachers simply don't have the time or freedom to do such progressive things.

The financial ramifications of education reform are also damaging schools around the country. As mentioned previously, funding for public education has declined. According to the Center on Budget and Policy Priorities:

States' new budgets are providing less per-pupil funding for kindergarten through 12th grade than they did six years ago – often far less. The reduced levels reflect not only the lingering effects of the 2007-09 recession but also continued austerity in many states; indeed, despite some improvements in overall state revenues, schools in around a third of states are entering the new school year with less state funding than they had last year. At a time when states and the nation are trying to produce workers with the skills to master new technologies and adapt to the complexities of a global economy, this decline in state educational investment is cause for concern. [35]

The phrase "trying to produce workers ..." diminishes my enthusiasm for the Center's point of view, but the facts are alarming nonetheless. The reasons for the decline are complex, including the "lingering effects of the recession" they cite. But this trend will continue despite the clear economic recovery. In part this is because the tide of "economic recovery" has floated all the luxury liners – but not so much the middle class rowboats.

As mentioned earlier, most schools are still funded by a stagnant or shrinking property tax base. Finally, and although this is a relatively small factor, according to the U.S. Census Bureau, the percentage of households in America with children under age 18 has been in steady decline, so too many of our citizens see education as someone else's problem.

These economic factors are exacerbated by the constant political rhetoric, which is parroted by educational reformers and conservative commentators. These bullet points are all false, yet they control much of the public debate about education, resulting in a widespread belief that schools don't really need more resources:

- Money doesn't fix education – we spend more than (choose your nation) and get worse results;

- Class size doesn't matter;

- Teachers are overpaid and don't even work all year;

- Teachers unions are only interested in the status quo and ripping off the rest of us;

- The reason that schools are bad is because parents are irresponsible – "It's their problem. I'm not paying to raise their (usually black) kids."

The fascination with economy of scale and the use of technology also contributes to the erosion of funding. If folks believe that technology can make education leaner and meaner, they certainly have a point. Schools have indeed gotten leaner and meaner.

Most of all, the rise of charter schools, the mirage of school "choice," and the hundreds of millions spent by hedge funds and foundations to fund a very small percentage of America's schools, create the illusion that we don't need a strong base of public funding for the public school system. The strategy of reformers seems to be to starve public schools of the funding they need so that increasing numbers of families will flee to the charters and voucher-funded private schools.

Because of destructive testing practices and the erosion of public school funding, educational reform has made many public schools worse and is decimating the ranks of America's professional teachers.

Damaging and Flawed Assessments of Children

The testing, grading and ranking of students is a nearly universal and accepted practice.

I recall a very unpleasant encounter with a parent, many years ago. The parent, not surprisingly a father, confronted me at an evening school event, arguing strenuously against our no-grades policy in Lower and Middle School. His son was in 3rd grade. He was still on the safe side of apoplectic when I asked him why he thought letter grades were so important. "I want to know how my boy is doing! What's wrong with that?"

"Nothing," I responded. "But how could you not know how he is doing? We provide several very comprehensive narrative reports each year. Each teacher writes extensively about his progress, his areas of slower growth – much more detail than I ever got about my kids when they were that age. We have several teacher-parent conferences during the year, when you can explore in depth the progress and growth of your son. And, as you are aware, we are very open and relaxed about communication and I hope you feel free to meet with any of his teachers if you are concerned."

Rather than being mollified by my reassurances, he apparently found them wanting, as his skin tone was quickly moving through pink toward livid. I will say, he had good neck veins. "But that's not the same! I want to know what his grades are!"

I responded, gently enough, "Why?"

"Because I want to know how he's doing compared to the other kids!!!"

Still gently, I asked, "Now why is that so important to you?"

End of conversation and, not too long after, the end of enrollment for his son.

I suppose this represents part of my philosophical concern. I don't find arranging students in a hierarchy of test grades a useful way of looking at children. I don't think it's good for the kids at the bottom (or the top and middle, for that matter). Education is not a competitive sport. Education is about learning and growing, not about winning and losing.

Many seem to believe that competition is an important, indispensable ingredient in a fine school. I suppose the former Calhoun parent quoted above held that view. Most progressive educators believe education is a cooperative enterprise, not a competitive one. As I will explicate in greater detail later, the extrinsic motivation stirred up in a highly competitive environment is ultimately less effective, and certainly less enjoyable, than the intrinsic motivation that starts with innate curiosity and grows into passion. Competition breeds attitudes and behavior in school that do not lead to rich intellectual development or healthy emotional growth.

Grades and grading degrade relationships between teachers and students. Warm, supportive relationships are the medium in which learning best flourishes.

Imagine the following – you enter a couple's exercise with your spouse, partner or good friend. The purpose is to deepen and improve your relationship through honest communication, a mutual assessment for growth. Each of you prepares a thoughtful inventory of the things you most love, respect and admire about the other. That's the easy part. Then, with requisite tact, you craft a second list – the things you wish your counterpart would examine, ways they might become an even more delightful partner. If done well, such a process might be both affirming and challenging – dynamics of value in any relationship. Stagnant water breeds disease.

Now imagine that your facilitator requires that you accompany your assessment with a letter grade. You must weigh the complex matrix of assets and liabilities and assign an A, B or C to your partner. (If you are drawn toward D or F, perhaps the process is too little, too late!) Furthermore, you are to calibrate your letter grade on a bell curve of desirable human traits as they occur in the population. Two outcomes are likely – an easy "A," which is dishonest and renders the assessment meaningless, or "I love you dearly, but I'm afraid you're a 'B-,' especially in light of other men I've known," an assessment not likely to enhance the relationship!

In a discussion several years ago about grades and grading, a thoughtful Upper School teacher offered the following characterization. After having reflected on and written a narrative about the progress, breakthroughs, stalls and frustrations of a particular student he would – and I love the phrase – "Slap a grade on it."

Assigning (slapping) grades, particularly when exacerbated by GPAs and class ranks, does several things. As Jerome Bruner argued, it conditions children to view learning as a process to determine what the teacher wants. This conditioning leads to risk-aversion and a phenomenon I call "learning to the test." The phrase "teaching to the test" is now common vernacular and properly identifies a powerful negative influence on education. But "learning to the test" is equally limiting and pervasive.

Even at a progressive school like Calhoun, despite teachers' best intentions, many students will ask, "Will it be on the test?" as a way of determining how they will spend time and intellectual energy.

This alone should prompt reconsideration of letter grades, but my concerns are more about the relationships we have with our students.

I teach journalism each year. Some students' work is technically fastidious but unimaginative. Does fastidious deserve an "A" in the absence of imagination or originality? Can eccentric brilliance deserve an "A" if it's riddled with punctuation errors? I want to affirm and challenge both the fastidious student and the creative student. Does my nearly arbitrary choice of a letter grade interfere with the affirmation and the challenge? I think so. Why is it not sufficient that I have an honest conversation with each student about these things without "slapping a grade on it?"

Take the example of a particularly interesting student several years ago whose originality was in rarified "A+" territory. Her prose was tortured and wandering. Grammar was not her strength. But her writing had shards of brilliance in every paragraph. It felt impossible to give her an "A," given the deep flaws in her technique. But it seemed a betrayal of our relationship to give her anything less. I'd have preferred to simply tell her both things honestly and supportively without having to characterize her as a "B."

The idea of grading and ranking is deeply embedded in our cultural understanding of school. That doesn't make it right. Letter grades do more to inhibit real learning than to inspire it. This claim is supported by the research looking at intrinsic and extrinsic motivation, as I describe in Chapter 4. There is no extrinsic structure more ubiquitous than letter grades in schools.

Testing and grading are also flawed by virtue of their standard expectations. Standard, grade-level expectations simply don't align with children's actual development. This renders any test, particularly of younger children, incapable of measuring their mastery or ability in a subject area.

Whether letter grades within a classroom or standardized test grades on a local, state, federal, or international exam, the results for any individual are relatively meaningless and possibly damaging. This is exacerbated by the test process itself, which can produce stress, punish kids who are naturally and delightfully distractible, and make it more about their ability to perform under pressure than any demonstration of knowledge or skill.

An arguably greater flaw in most assessment schemes is that they are inextricably wed to the "uniform" approach that Howard Gardner warned against several decades ago. In both school grades and standardized tests, there is an implicit bias and explicit privilege given to linguistic and logical-mathematical intelligences. Since Gardner's notion of multiple intelligences has been affirmed by neurobiology, can any grading or testing scheme be reasonable if it disproportionately addresses only those two limited aspects of intelligence?

This bias plays out in direct, unambiguous ways. It is self-evident, for example, that logical-mathematical intelligence is a great asset in taking a mathematics exam. This intelligence is also an asset in many science courses. This is particularly true, for example, if a science course, a physics curriculum for example, and its examinations are primarily or entirely based on manipulating algorithms.

It is also self-evident that linguistic intelligence is the area being assessed in most English examinations and essays. Linguistic intelligence is also the currency in most other humanities assessments. Assessment in history generally requires a significant amount of decoding and encoding – writing, reading, and interpreting – all within the linguistic realm. Other humanities courses also resort to assessment through linguistic intelligence. In an Art History course, for example, a student's understanding of aesthetic matters will be tested with linguistic intelligence as a gatekeeper, no matter how profound his/her ability to perceive and/or create beauty.

I'll stipulate for a moment that this bias toward logical-mathematical and linguistic intelligence is reasonably fair in a mathematics or English exam. But where in teaching or assessment are the other ways of being intelligent given fair acknowledgment?

Good teachers often do some of this in the teaching part of their work. Intrapersonal and interpersonal intelligences offer an advantage when students work in groups, a process that can construct more powerful learning than any one individual on their own. Certainly the capacity for empathy and insight, sensitivity and compassion, can lead to a much richer understanding of a great novel or a dynamic period in human history. A mathematics or science concept may be more accurately and helpfully presented in ways that a student who has visual-spatial strength will understand, perhaps more fully than a logical-mathematical peer. In my experience at Landmark College, I watched students with profound dyslexia learn essay structure through dance. I could offer many, many other examples of teaching in ways that recognize multiple intelligences.

But the more salient point is that even when good teaching occurs, the assessments/tests still revert to the linguistic and logical-mathematical intelligences almost exclusively. This privileges the two historic intelligences, disadvantages the students whose intelligence strengths lie elsewhere, and renders the assessments unfair and incomplete.

It doesn't have to be this way. Calhoun and many other progressive schools have very few conventional examinations. A literature class may allow a student to show mastery by making a film. Rather than final exams, we have demonstration days. Students build things, debate, and draw graphical representations of physical and mathematical concepts. I'm not suggesting that a progressive school should not value a luminous essay or an elegant solution to a complex calculus problem. I'm suggesting that these should not be the only demonstrations of intelligence or mastery that are honored.

Before moving on to the more destructive and widespread testing that has taken over public education, a brief digression on speed – and I don't mean the methamphetamines used by highly stressed college students! Where did the idea come from that speed is important? We've all heard the starting command, "Pick up your pencils!" and the more troubling, "Time's up. Put down your pencils!" Most assessments in most schools are timed. Why? Is a problem solved in 15 minutes a less worthy achievement than a problem solved in 10 minutes? Does an essay written in two hours have greater value than the same, or better, essay that took four hours to craft?

When in a school environment – primary, secondary, post-secondary, graduate, post-graduate – ask the teacher, proctor, professor why the exam is being timed so ferociously. What exactly is being measured and what is at stake? Is it because we simply value brutish efficiency? Is it because we think taking time, reflecting and reconsidering, are qualities to be extinguished? I'd be really curious to hear the answers, because I really can't imagine what they might be. If no intelligent rationale is forthcoming, perhaps we can begin removing speed as an important variable in assessing the value of students and their work.

The issue of standardized testing is exceedingly complex. I've addressed several of the fundamental flaws above. Just as with grading and testing in daily school practice, standardized testing regimens make no sense when they are designed with the expectation that all children are at the same developmental stage and have the same mix of intelligences. Standardized tests are also a potent manifestation of the extrinsic motivation system that plagues education.

On an individual basis, children are being judged unfairly, with real and ongoing consequences to their sense of self. Families and caregivers are alarmed and discouraged if a child doesn't do well. Summer school or other remediation can also be prescribed, further eroding self-worth and self-confidence and detracting from more important and more enjoyable aspects of childhood.

The consequences of the aggregate results may be worse. Schools are deemed "failing," teachers are losing their jobs, cheating scandals are frequent, schools are wasting inordinate amounts of valuable student time on test preparation, and a whole industry of charter schools, voucher programs and private educational management organizations is emerging.

Put aside for a moment that these tests are developmentally unfair and tend to measure only a small fraction of the abilities any particular child possesses at any given point in time. Let's stipulate that the aggregate results measure something important about children's progress in mathematics and language arts. How's the testing and accountability era working?

Not so well.

The 2001 No Child Left Behind Law (NCLB) promised to have all students "succeeding" by 2014. By December 2014 overall performance on standardized tests had not improved at all, indicating something much less than universal success. In a few places, New York City for example, periodic claims were made in the previous decade that scores showed progress. On closer examination, the claims were false or, in several cases, a result of changing the standard for passing the tests.

It would be a very difficult logistical challenge to quantify the precise effect of 13 years of constant testing on student performance, because both the testing instruments and the standards for interpreting results have shifted throughout the period. But whether there has been no change or there has been marginal improvement in test results, there has been a decided decline in actual learning.

The primary problem with assessing the impact of testing and accountability on achievement is that the process is a closed loop. The desired outcomes (correct answers on tests) have been predetermined and, therefore, the educational process has been engineered to achieve those outcomes. In common parlance, this is "teaching to the test." This process should, by logical inference, lead to higher scores, whether or not the scores are meaningful. For example, if we agreed that the indicator of great progress in language would be the ability to get more answers right on a vocabulary test, then we might spend the day – every day – learning and drilling vocabulary lists. It would not be surprising, in this somewhat hypothetical case, to see more and more students getting more and more answers right on the vocabulary test.

In a slightly more complicated way, this is precisely what is happening in conventional public education. The desired outcomes are clearly stated. Teaching, in the most rote, unimaginative ways, is directed toward achieving those outcomes. Then tests, most developed by the multinational Pearson Publishing Corporation, assess whether students have reached the desired outcomes. This self-fulfilling process should, by rational deduction, result in improvements in test scores, just as in my hypothetical vocabulary exercise above. But that hasn't happened. The failure of the standards and accountability era has been blamed on everyone and everything but the real culprit. Teachers are under assault. Principals are fired. Teachers unions are at fault. Bad parenting must be the cause.

The real culprit? The process itself. The "drill and kill" practices of the testing and accountability era are guaranteed to inhibit children's ability to do well on subsequent tests. It is a self-fulfilling prophecy of failure.

What about the success stories? The highly publicized schools, often charters, where standardized test scores have reportedly gone up?

Many well-informed critics have debunked most of the claims. There is significant evidence that the more "successful" schools have lower proportions of students with learning disabilities and fewer students with other than English as a first language. Excluding these lower scoring students from the testing pool will raise both the mean and median test scores. And the attrition rates of many "successful" schools are very high, indicating that they jettison kids who might soil their statistics.

Even accounting for this sleight of hand, let's agree that some schools, including the highly praised Knowledge Is Power Program (KIPP) schools, actually raise test scores. Many of these so-called high performing charter schools are more like miniature military schools. They have much longer school hours, a fact they boast about. Many have school on Saturdays and through most of the summer. They relentlessly and efficiently drill the kids. They claim that this is the price that must be paid for achievement – for the upward mobility that so many parents long for in the most neglected communities in America. So, is it worth it?

I believe the answer is unequivocally and emphatically "No!"

The price would be too high even if the test results were meaningful, which they are not. Unlike the majority of public schools, where no test score progress has been made, these schools have at least fulfilled the self-fulfilling prophecy. By gritty determination, strict discipline and long hours they have drilled the kids on the things that will be tested, and so the kids get more answers right. But they haven't really learned much at all.

There is an entire academic industry devoted to the assessment of students and to the analysis of various types of schools, curriculum, and pedagogy. Unfortunately, economists do a great deal of this work. It sometimes seems that we live in an economy, not a society. The analyses done by economists are cited by reformers and accepted without examination by education writers and politicians. Opponents of school reform are often characterized as politically motivated obstructionists, beholden to the status quo, servants to recalcitrant unions, and enemies of progress. "Look," the reformers say, "the research proves that reform is working."

One such example is the work of the University of Michigan's Susan Dynarski. She and various colleagues, economists all, have published a number of scholarly papers demonstrating the efficacy of charter schools. One such paper, "Inputs and Impacts in Charter Schools: KIPP Lynn," [36] was published in the May 2010 issue of the *American Economic Review*. I don't mean to pick on Professor Dynarski. I'm sure she is a capable economist and there are many others who have done similar work. The paper to which I refer probably represents a careful and comprehensive statistical analysis of the "outcomes" achieved in this one KIPP School. I will credit Dynarski et al. with one thing, the final sentence in the paper, "Our results suggest the major elements of this model combine to produce noteworthy achievement gains, at least as measured on state-wide standardized tests."

The final phrase is the most important, with emphasis on "at least." The results she affirms are meaningless without context. A group of economists, however sincere, are not equipped to assess the broad consequences of the program imposed on children in KIPP schools. As argued earlier, the self-fulfilling, closed loop of testing and teaching to the test doesn't prove anything at all. In any isolated context, one will find improvement when narrowly defining desired outcomes and then designing repetitive activities directed to achieving those outcomes. The arcane statistical methods and technical language used by these economists lends hefty credibility to what is a lightweight analysis.

A more accurate assessment of the impact of rote, conventional methodology is found in a 2013 report from the Massachusetts Institute of Technology (MIT). MIT neuroscientists studied 1,400 eighth graders in Boston schools. [37] The findings were unambiguous and not surprising to any progressive educator. Students who achieved higher scores on standardized tests showed no improvement in what the researchers call "fluid intelligence." Fluid intelligence is a broad term used to describe critical thinking capacity, the ability to innovate or solve novel problems – in short, qualities that are most valuable in life, work and higher education. It is ironic that the MIT report was co-authored with an individual who also co-authored Dynarski's so-called "proof of efficacy."

The results for so-called "high performing" charter schools were particularly striking:

> *Even stronger evidence came from a comparison of about 200 students who had entered a lottery for admittance to a handful of Boston's oversubscribed charter schools, many of which achieve strong improvement in MCAS scores. The researchers found that students who were randomly selected to attend high-performing charter schools did significantly better on the math MCAS than those who were not chosen, but there was no corresponding increase in fluid intelligence scores.*

Even some of the charter schools have admitted confusion. Many schools with the highest test scores and highest graduation rates have found that their graduates struggle in college, with failure rates as high as 80%. These kids have not learned in the true and deep meaning of the word, and are overwhelmed when presented with novel problems, the need for critical thinking, or the ability to adapt to the complex expectations of higher education. Marginal improvements on standardized tests come with great costs – rigid, suffocating conformity, demeaning discipline, suppression of curiosity, loss of freedom, and loss of childhood.

Here's my simple economic analysis of KIPP and other charters – the price is too high and the product is too flimsy.

None of this has diminished the influence of the testing industry or the zeal of the metrics and accountability advocates. In the wake of the failure of NCLB, policy makers, having learned nothing from the dismal failure, stuck to their guns, and shifted the semantics while leaving the testing and accountability requirements essentially unchanged. Race to the Top (RTTT) became the law of the land. RTTT applied financial leverage to drive states further into the metrics morass. Recent legislation at both federal and state levels requires accountability and test-score-based teacher evaluations in order to receive critical funding. Districts or schools who don't play nice with educational reform can find themselves in precarious financial straits.

A potent brew of federal policy and philanthropic arm-twisting presses legislatures to authorize more charter schools under the banner of "choose your school, just like the rich folks!" This educational reform propaganda is nonsense. The private schools where privileged parents send their kids are expensive and highly selective. I know. I'm the Head of one of them. Calhoun's tuition is an embarrassing $48,000 per year – about average for Manhattan private schools.

Poor families in New York City don't have the "choice" to attend Calhoun or any of the other private schools. At Calhoun we offer a great deal of tuition assistance so that our students are not all from wealthy families, but the glib come-on-in support of privatization is inaccurate and dishonest. Try taking a $5,000 to $7,000 voucher to a place like Sidwell Friends, where the Obamas sent their daughters. Sidwell's tuition is also about $40,000. They too offer generous tuition assistance for some of the few students they select from among thousands of applicants, but the political rhetoric is disingenuous.

School choice primarily diverts public funds to religious schools, not to schools like Calhoun or Sidwell Friends. In North Carolina, 90% of the vouchers are used for religious school attendance, in Florida, 82%. The Anti-Defamation League estimates that 80% of voucher recipients nationwide use them for religious schools. [38] School choice is a catchy euphemism for a campaign to eviscerate public education and replace it with a hodgepodge of charter school chains, online programs, pop-up storefronts, and publicly supported religious schools.

RTTT has not yielded any of the desired outcomes either, so now the political and financial attention has turned to the Common Core. The Common Core is both boon and boondoggle. Boon to the publishing industry – Pearson and other corporations reportedly stand to earn hundreds of millions of dollars – and a political boondoggle in that angry objection to the Common Core seems to be the only issue in America that has bipartisan support. Conservatives don't want the government to have any role in education and liberals don't want government to play this particular role either.

The Common Core and its tests also reduce learning to a dismal process, guaranteed to turn off children and unfairly assess their intellectual capabilities. In mid-2014, New York's Education Commissioner, John B. King, Jr. sought support for the Common Core by releasing a large sample of actual test questions. If it weren't so serious, it would be hilarious. The Commissioner evidently believed that a review of this material would convince teachers and critics that the Common Core, its implementation, and its related testing are wise and wonderful. King, a great fan of the Common Core, is now Arne Duncan's successor at the Department of Education. His blog post, since deleted, was titled "Our Students. Their Moment", but the sample questions were in fact released in August, 2014. [39] I rebutted this post and provided a critique of one of the Grade 3 English Language Arts (ELA) questions with a blog post of my own I called "Our Students. Their Moment. My A**!" [40] Here's an excerpt:

> *The very first third-grade ELA section amply demon-*
> *strates the absurdity of the entire scheme. Students are*
> *asked to read a relatively innocuous piece titled "Sugaring*
> *Time." It is a straightforward description of the process*
> *through which maple syrup is produced. The intentions*
> *are laughably transparent throughout this dull exercise.*
> *I can just imagine a freshly minted MBA and a Teach*
> *for America alumna sitting in a Pearson cubicle saying,*
> *"Good education is student-centered, right? Kids like*
> *maple syrup, don't they? Great idea!" The first sentence of*
> *"Sugaring Time" – "You probably like to eat maple syrup*
> *on your pancakes and waffles, right?"*
>
> *Yummy! This test will really be fun!*

The essay is presented in short chunks, probably because the Teach for America graduate had a brain-biology seminar during her several weeks of training. Each chunk is numbered, so as to allow easy reference when the kids look back and try to figure out which one of the several plausible multiple-choice answers they should select. A junior-sized SAT.

A less developed third grader on the Upper West Side scratches his head in confusion, squirms in his chair and gives up. The words on the page, which had initially been mildly interesting, become an incomprehensible blur. A more developed third grader in Westchester County wastes 10 minutes pondering the reasons that three of the proposed answers might be right. The pondering leads to anxiety, which leads in turn to the student gazing longingly out the window at a real maple tree, wishing she could be climbing it. Thousands of third graders in the South Bronx don't know or care about maple syrup, since it costs $20 a pint. It's like having an SAT question about a 1982 Chateau Haut-Brion.

I'm essentially a Vermonter, despite living and working in New York. I love maple syrup so much that I could pour it on broccoli. I never believed that anything could make me averse to maple syrup. But I was wrong. It may take months before I can look at a can of "Grade A Light Amber (Fancy)." New Englanders should object to the Common Core just on the basis of its potential to disrupt the local economy.

Using maple syrup to draw little moths to the flame of testing and accountability is philosophically offensive.

The whole mess is philosophically offensive. Anyone who understands child development – nay, anyone who was actually a child and remembers it – knows that curiosity is as natural as sap from a maple tree. Kids want to learn, unless we make it dull and frustrating.

Here's a radical idea! Why not take the class to a sugar bush in upstate New York, let them tap a tree, taste the sap, visit the sugarhouse and watch the process of making syrup? Then invite them to write a journal entry about it. I suppose that doesn't correspond to one of the Common Core standards.

I intended to review dozens of the ELA and math questions so that I could craft a well-informed critique. I just couldn't. I got through the first three or four and my eyes glazed over. I'm heading up to Vermont soon. I suppose I'll just butter my pancakes.

Can we really develop an agile, probing intellect by making children choose from among a set of possible conclusions crafted by the test developers at Pearson Publishing? The testing and accountability approach to intellectual complexity and beauty is enough to make any reasonable child hate school. And that's what education reform is doing in America. Making education absurd and unpleasant.

David Coleman, the man considered the architect of the Common Core, is now President of the College Board, the organization with a stranglehold on the secondary school-to-college pipeline. Observers note that he, in complicity with many others, has created a cradle-to-grave monopoly on student assessment. The Common Core objectives align beautifully with the College Board's APs, SATs, GREs and other college gatekeeping exams.

Coleman also thinks the current investment in testing is insufficient. Speaking at the Brookings Institute in 2012 he offered the elegant observation that current policy is "... making testing shorter and shittier." [41] This is a bit like the CEO of McDonalds bemoaning a declining market share for Big Macs. In the estimation of the testing industry, there can never be enough of a bad, profitable thing.

If grades and other extrinsic structures are not a good way to assess kids, and standardized measures are inherently flawed and drive bad educational practices, what should our policies and practices be? Isn't it important to assess how our students are doing? Shouldn't our teachers and schools be accountable to parents and taxpayers? Shouldn't critics like me come up with solutions rather than just complaining?

Here's a solution. Pay teachers the professional salaries the importance of their work merits. Support schools so that class sizes are 15 or less. Give teachers the time, resources and autonomy to know and respond to each child they teach, rather than divert their energies to test preparation or content "coverage." Given the chance, most teachers could fully assess every student every day with complex, thoughtful, human acuity. They could, but they don't, because the demands of today's uniform, standardized, accountability-obsessed policies leave little time for them to actually be teachers.

Howard Gardner was prescient in 1993 when he wrote:

Yet I am equally convinced that many of the cures suggested by neoconservative reformers are worse than the disease; and that in any case the proposed cures will

*not heal the patients. My fundamental quarrel with the
uniform comes with my conviction that it is based on a
fundamentally flawed view of human cognition – one that
I call 'IQ-style thinking.'* [9]

Here we are, some 22 years later, with a highly profitable
and deeply entrenched system of assessment that is, as Gardner
bemoaned, "based on a fundamentally flawed view of human
cognition." And, I would add, on a fundamentally flawed view
of natural human development and neurobiology.

Chapter Three

Technology – Blessing or Curse?

A Romantic Interlude

Understanding progressive education requires making a clear distinction between life and the symbolic representation of life. The central principles of progressive education have always including learning through real, natural, human experiences.

Although it is not a new phenomenon, conventional schools and their students have become increasing awash in symbols and less immersed in real life. Children are decoding symbols on a page or a device, sounding out each letter as Dick and Jane go for a walk or Jack and Jill go up the hill and fetch some water. Later they will read chapter books and take quizzes on the characters' names. In high school they might read *Catcher in the Rye* and identify with Holden Caulfield as he navigates adolescence. With good humor, I have to point out that J.D. Salinger might have never written *Catcher in the Rye* had he not suffered through a decidedly conventional experience at Valley Forge Military Academy. I suppose his great book can be considered the pearl formed out of his deeply irritating education.

But, of course, symbols are not the only thing. Stories, particularly the printed or digitized ones, are merely the symbolic representation of real human experience. While there is indeed a vicarious benefit to readers, a good book is no substitute for a good life. Salinger himself was a sad example of this, as his life was apparently bitter and lonely, with the symbolic report of his adolescent misery as the only important artifact.

This excerpt about music from Paul Lockhart's marvelous essay, *A Mathematician's Lament*, [42] is a satirical example of the limits of symbolic emphasis, but not so far from the truth:

> *A musician wakes from a terrible nightmare. In his dream he finds himself in a society where music education has been made mandatory. "We are helping our students become more competitive in an increasingly sound-filled world." Educators, school systems, and the state are put in charge of this vital project. Studies are commissioned, committees are formed, and decisions are made – all without the advice or participation of a single working musician or composer.*

> *Since musicians are known to set down their ideas in the form of sheet music, these curious black dots and lines must constitute the "language of music." It is imperative that students become fluent in this language if they are to attain any degree of musical competence; indeed, it would*

be ludicrous to expect a child to sing a song or play an instrument without having a thorough grounding in music notation and theory. Playing and listening to music, let alone composing an original piece, are considered very advanced topics and are generally put off until college, and more often graduate school.

As for the primary and secondary schools, their mission is to train students to use this language – to jiggle symbols around according to a fixed set of rules: "Music class is where we take out our staff paper, our teacher puts some notes on the board, and we copy them or transpose them into a different key. We have to make sure to get the clefs and key signatures right, and our teacher is very picky about making sure we fill in our quarter-notes completely. One time we had a chromatic scale problem and I did it right, but the teacher gave me no credit because I had the stems pointing the wrong way."

In their wisdom, educators soon realize that even very young children can be given this kind of musical instruction. In fact it is considered quite shameful if one's third-grader hasn't completely memorized his circle of fifths. "I'll have to get my son a music tutor. He simply won't apply himself to his music homework. He says it's boring. He just sits there staring out the window, humming tunes to himself and making up silly songs."

In the higher grades the pressure is really on. After all, the students must be prepared for the standardized tests and college admissions exams. Students must take courses in Scales and Modes, Meter, Harmony, and Counterpoint. "It's a lot for them to learn, but later in college when they finally get to hear all this stuff, they'll really appreciate all the work they did in high school." Of course, not many students actually go on to concentrate in music, so only a few will ever get to hear the sounds that the black dots represent. Nevertheless, it is important that every member of society be able to recognize a modulation or a fugal passage, regardless of the fact that they will never hear one. "To tell you the truth, most students just aren't very good at music. They are bored in class, their skills are terrible, and their homework is barely legible. Most of them couldn't care less about how important music is in today's world; they just want to take the minimum number of music courses and be done with it. I guess there are just music people and non-music people. I had this one kid, though, man was she sensational! Her sheets were impeccable – every note in the right place, perfect calligraphy, sharps, flats, just beautiful. She's going to make one hell of a musician someday."

Waking up in a cold sweat, the musician realizes, gratefully, that it was all just a crazy dream. "Of course!" he reassures himself, "No society would ever reduce such a beautiful and meaningful art form to something so mindless and trivial; no culture could be so cruel to its children as to deprive them of such a natural, satisfying means of human expression. How absurd!"

Trying to create musicians by having them read and write notes on a page is a dry, meaningless activity. If one hopes to spawn a great cellist, have your child listen to Bach's unaccompanied cello suites – in a great recital hall, if possible. For the nascent musician, the resonance of the instrument, the eternal power of the composition and the commitment of the performer just might ignite a passion to learn how to do that. Pick up a cello and draw the bow across the strings. Smell the rosin. Listen to the deep, penetrating sound. Then, of course, it takes practice, practice, practice, which is, as we all know, the way to Carnegie Hall. But exposure to the beauty must come first.

If you hope to raise an astronomer, emulate Wendy Mogel and her friends [5], naked on a rooftop in childhood. If you wish, skip the naked part, but let your child view the Milky Way and dream about the moon. If you hope your child might be a great scientist, let her loose in the woods for hours every day. The greatest irony of a conventional, uniform approach to education is that it deprives children of the very experiences that are conveyed in the symbolic notations they are supposed to care about!

The representation of real experience in symbolic notation is equally limiting in mathematics and science. We have been conditioned to believe that math is the symbols we memorize and regurgitate. That misperception is part of Lockhart's lamentation. But take a simple example, the computation $4 + 3 = 7$. The numbers actually represent something true. The symbols themselves are just shorthand. The idea of $4 + 3 = 7$ is more accurately portrayed as 4 apples and 3 oranges, which combined in a bowl, are 7 discrete objects. The apples and oranges are the mathematical truth. The algorithms of algebra, geometry, calculus and physics are humankind's best efforts to symbolically represent something that is true in the physical universe.

That may seem obvious, but its relevance to education is very important. In the simplest example, allowing a student to manipulate the oranges and apples is a much better way of internalizing the mathematical idea of $4 + 3$. It may be more fun too, but it invites other senses into what is otherwise a purely abstract, symbolic exercise. When playing with the fruit, children are using tactile information and 3-dimensional, visual information. They might even use a sense of smell to divide the sum into its parts. In every aspect of science and mathematics, exposure to the actual thing is of tremendous importance in the development of understanding the symbolic representation.

In distinguishing between symbolic and real I'm reminded of an old, silly joke.

An eager student, Emily, signs up for her first foray into theater. She, fortunately, has a very minor role. In the midst of a dramatic war sequence she is to cry out, "Hark, the cannons roar!" Emily rehearses the line for hours at home, asking parents, grandparents and a very irritated older brother to listen. Back at school she performs flawlessly in each rehearsal. On cue, at precisely the moment called for in the script, she shouts, "Hark, the cannons roar!"

Finally, opening night arrives. Her parents, grandparents and a very reluctant older brother are in the audience. She is resplendent in costume and stage make-up. Her excitement (and theirs, except for the brother) is palpable. The long anticipated moment nears. Flushed with excitement, she stands stage left, awaiting her debut. Just as she is about to recite her well-rehearsed line the tech theater guys set off the backstage cannon. BOOM!!!!! Emily flinches, looks around and asks, loudly, "What the hell was that?"

When schools fail to attend to the different ways in which children are intelligent, when they fail to fill the school with a rich array of sensory information, when they immerse children in the symbolic representation of life rather than life itself, children are likely to leave school, encounter beautiful, fascinating things and say, "What the hell is that?"

The Curse of Technology

One of the fun traditions at Calhoun is Grandparents Day. It has become even more fun since I became a grandparent. On one Grandparents Day a grinning grandpa stopped to chat with me for a minute, doing what all grandparents do – bragging about his grandchild. His grandson is truly the best child in the world, as are yours and mine. It is a human reality that defies mathematical analysis. But it was the nature of his brag that stood out. "My grandson," he said while puffing his chest out, "really knows how to operate the computer." His grandson was three at the time. It was not an occasion to pierce his puff with a lecture, so I smiled, nodded and said nothing at all.

This is a common point of view, especially among those of a certain age. I assume this gent was born in the 40s and has an understandably high regard for "the computer." In the 1950s a UNIVAC computer, its vacuum tubes and wires, filled a room the size of a small gym. "Operating" that computer was no mean feat. My father was a mathematician/engineer at IBM, and then in 1955 he started the computing center at the Case Institute of Technology, now part of Case Western Reserve University. I spent hours in the company of UNIVAC, running punch cards through the sorter and marveling at the complexity and mystery of it all. Until the advent of the personal computer, anyone who could "operate a computer" was rightly seen as bright and capable. To this Calhoun grandpa, his grandson was a budding Alan Turing.

But today, operating a computer is only slightly more complex than turning on the television. (Actually, not. My cable remote is slightly more complex than my MacBook Air!) It's like a grandfather at a Grandparents Day in 1955 bursting with pride, "My grandson can operate the television!" By today's understanding, a room full of televisions in a school would hardly be seen as fine education unless you are Chris Whittle, the Edison Schools guy who brought the world Channel One, which is the contemporary equivalent of that room full of televisions.

I'm no Luddite. I didn't write this book with quill and inkpot and I have more Apple devices than apples in my house, a source of some shame. Yes, advances in technology are very helpful.

There are ways that technology can genuinely enliven education. Many schools use simulations that bring important concepts into vivid relief. Using technology to interact with and learn from children in other parts of the world can be a powerful experience. Technology eases the burden of any number of routine tasks, freeing us to use time in more interesting and effective ways. And the amount of available information is astonishing and useful, as long as it is consumed with a critical cognitive palate.

My objections to technology are mostly directed to the misuse with young children and to the alarming tendency to substitute technology for real human interaction.

Many books and scholarly articles question the efficacy of and warn about the risks of the digital neighborhood. You can find them via Google on your mobile device. (I add that as ironic acknowledgment of the two edges of the technology sword.) One brilliant skeptic, to whom I referred earlier, is Jane

Healy, Ph.D., and grandmother of a former Calhoun student. Her books, *Endangered Minds: Why Children Don't Think And What We Can Do About It* [43] and *Failure to Connect: How Computers Affect Our Children's Minds – and What We Can Do About It* [44], are good summaries of why all parents and educators should be skeptical about technology. Healy both warns and corrects, making suggestions for balanced and appropriate use of technology in schools and homes.

I think Healy and others concede too much, but I suppose the technological craze is not going away. While it is not my central point, and I won't belabor it, I believe children and schools would be just fine without any computers at all – at least until late middle school or high school. The idea that we need to teach computing to kids is absurd, given the clever and manipulative explosion of user-friendly software and hardware. The average toddler can figure most of it out by herself (and her grandparents will be very proud).

The hazards of technology for young kids were clear enough in 1990 when Healy wrote *Endangered Minds,* and the evidence has mounted ever since. I needn't thoroughly explicate the risks here, but there are serious concerns about the effects of digital exposure on young brains such as truncating attention span, decline in analytic ability, less developed verbal expression, stunted ability to solve complex problems, and others. Healy argues that in the course of brain development, certain groups of neurons are especially ripe for stimulation from various types of active learning. Missing these windows of opportunity by sitting in front of screens may create permanent deficits. But her book and other evidence from psychology and neurobiology are feeble Davids in a fight against the Goliath tech industry and its education handmaidens.

I still get riled thinking about a Microsoft ad from years ago. It began with images of children in a desert, measuring cacti. The project, as I recall, was to examine the effect of rainfall on the circumference of cactus plants. That sounds like a good progressive piece of curriculum. But those 5 seconds of images faded to students at computer monitors, punching their measurements on a keyboard and producing brilliantly colored bar graphs and pie charts. They were, as children will be, enchanted with the professional looking presentations and vibrant images. The value in this educational experience was diminished by the technology. They would have learned more by staying in the desert, plotting their data with stubby pencils on graph paper, calculating the variables and then sleeping under the stars.

I've seen the same behavior in something as simple as an essay or news piece in my journalism class, where the writing is dashed off quickly so the student may experiment with different fonts, import cute graphic images, and play around with the latest widget on Word Press.

The latest educational fad is the enthusiasm to teach coding to children, including very young children. The argument, as is so often the case when looking at education as a vocational enterprise, is that coding is an indispensable skill in the 21st century economy. Coding is certainly a useful skill. Whether you view the digital age with awe or dread, the exchange of information and the operations of all sorts of things are dependent on someone, somewhere, producing billions of lines of code. But let it be someone other than children in schools. The world's greatest problem is not a shortage of people who can write computer code. Just how many "apps" does humanity need? Our challenge is to develop humans who have the fluid intellect, creativity, imagination, aesthetic sensibilities and ethical convictions to save the world from the sorry mess we have created. That's the purpose of education. Those who are deeply educated can easily find someone else to write the code that facilitates their vision for a better world.

Other hot topics in education in recent years include "blended learning" and "flipped classrooms." Technology is at the center of these contrivances. The concept, briefly, is to turn the home/school relationship upside down. Students get content and practice skills through on-line or digital sources, working on their own. Then classrooms – referred to as "brick and mortar" so as to make actual schools seem old-fashioned – are places where teachers individualize instruction through cyber-supervision. Both parts of this blended learning are highly dependent on technology. One such program provides teachers with a "dashboard," through which they can digitally observe each student's online behavior, sending online chat messages to "get on task" if the student's digital activity wanders from the assigned work. A great deal of time and money is devoted to digital feedback systems, metrics, analytics, data collection and assessment. Arlene Karidis, an education reporter, writes on *The Huffington Post* about teachers working 15 hours per day keeping up with the systems and data aspects of blended learning:

> *Faculty need to be tech-savvy as new tools are introduced to the classroom. They have to be versed in assessing volumes of digitally generated, real-time data on each student. And they must to be ready to change course fast to reinforce or reintroduce concepts, depending on what the data shows.* [45]

The argument for tech-skepticism is implicit in many of the

principles of progressive education. Relationships are central to learning, both as a contributor to the release of dopamine, but also as a critical social context for language development as articulated by Vygotsky, Bruner et al. The colorful images that often accompany education articles or on school websites show children sitting in small cubicles, smiling at their computers, with little human interaction at all. Computers merely simulate the various sensory experiences that attend to multiple intelligences. They don't engage children with the real physical universe. Computer programs only allow students to manipulate pre-determined variables, not to construct their own knowledge.

Digital engagement is addictive, as we all know too well. The constant bombardment of fast-moving images and information can habituate the brain in ways that inhibit other learning. In 2010, a great series of articles in *The New York Times* [46] by Matt Richtel and other reporters, titled "Your Brain on Computers", warned of many other ways technology may be more harmful than helpful. One of these pieces made a compelling case that constant digital engagement denies the brain the downtime necessary for consolidating information and creating memories.

Whether any one or all of these concerns are fully validated is somewhat beside the point. In the aggregate, they form a strong case for caution in the use of technology for children. If we stipulate that the risks are, at the very least, plausible, then there would have to be a very powerful reason to take those risks.

What is absent in the discussion of technology in schools is any proof of its value. Quite to the contrary, there is emerging evidence of the lack of value or, more accurately, the harm it causes. A January 2015 piece in *The New York Times* [47] by developmental psychologist Susan Pinker cited research done by Duke University. This longitudinal study tracked the academic performance of "disadvantaged middle-school students against the dates they were given networked computers." The results were as I would expect – "Students who gain access to a home computer between the 5th and 8th grades tend to witness a persistent decline in reading and math scores." This decline was persistent over five years and the decline was markedly steeper among poor, black students. The study demonstrates that enthusiasm for technology doesn't bring results even within the closed loop of teaching rote skills in order to improve test scores. In other words, the use of technology carries all the risks I have explicated and doesn't even balance that risk by improving the meaningless scores that are the currency of success in conventional education. So it's a lose-lose proposition.

Like the proud Calhoun grandfather, folks have faith in computers just because technology sounds important, and because technology companies spend hundreds of millions of dollars hawking their wares to schools. This is a verbatim copy of an email I received in early 2015 from Pearson Publishing:

Dear Administrator:

NCS Pearson, Inc. (Pearson) offers the opportunity for schools to inform the advancement of education and receive educational benefits to support student growth and learning. Educational benefits such as iPads, Kindle Fires, and Nook tablets. This exciting opportunity involves your school's participation in the Equivalency phase of one of Pearson's products, AIMSweb.

AIMSweb is a universal screening, progress monitoring, and data management system for grades K-12. AIMSweb utilizes general outcome measurement, a form of standardized assessment of basic academic skills that predict year-end proficiency and are highly sensitive to change. Measures are time efficient, easy to administer, and produce accurate charts of student growth over time.

This email is to inform you of our AIMSweb Math K-1 Equivalency Study that will be beginning within a couple of weeks. The study will begin on March 2nd, 2015 and will run up until March 31, 2015. If interested, I have attached an information letter that describes the test in further detail and a roster template. If you have any questions or concerns, please feel free to give us a call or simply reply to this email.

They seduce schools with the promise of more attention-sapping devices so that they can sell a costly standardized assessment tool, using cash strapped schools as guinea pigs.

The symbolic representation of life is not the same as life itself. Perhaps the greatest harm done by technology is an act of omission. Every hour of screen time, whether in school or at home, is an hour not spent in some much more important activity, especially those things that involve real human engagement.

But these neurobiological and psychological questions about digital immersion can't withstand the incessant press for automation and standardization. As has been my theme throughout, technology is just the most recent manifestation of the industrial model of education. Inherent in the technological model of education is economy of scale. It must be impersonal, and people and parts must be interchangeable. It must be replicable. It must be quick and efficient, and measurable with terabytes of data and clouds of metrics. Most importantly, it must be *profitable*.

Chapter Four

Natural Development of Children

A natural view of children and child development must account for individual variances in development. Consider the words "standard" and "standards." Anyone with children, or anyone who was once a child, knows that humans are anything but "standard." Yet nearly everything about the design of educational settings would have you believe otherwise. Grade level standards and expectations are ubiquitous in schools and education rhetoric. Grades themselves – 1st, 2nd etc., are organized around the notion that all children can and should do certain things at the same time and in the same way. This may seem like a reasonable way to arrange a school, but it has very little to do with real children. Abstract children can be neatly divided by age, but real children differ significantly from each other.

We not only ignore their differences, but we press them to

learn too early and too fast.

Years ago I attended a presentation by Wendy Mogel, author of *The Blessing of a Skinned Knee: Using Jewish Teachings to Raise Self-Reliant Children* [5]. Mogel reminisced fondly of childhood nights when she and her friends stuffed pillows into their nightgowns, slid them under the covers, and climbed naked onto the roof to feel cool breezes on bare bottoms and gaze with wonder at the night sky. In childhood I played baseball or football, climbed trees, or sneaked puffs from contraband cigarettes (disclaimer – we didn't know then what we know now!) with my friends, from school dismissal until nightfall. My parents had no idea where I was until I arrived, invariably filthy and late, for dinner. These days the neighbors would call child welfare.

Mogel urges parents to back off by invoking a lovely metaphor. She invites us to think of children as wildflower seeds in unlabeled packages. Sow the seeds, occasionally water, and expose to lots of sunshine. Children, like unlabeled wildflowers, will blossom early or late in myriad brilliant and subtle colors if we just give them enough time and support. All the pushing and worry in the world won't change a sky-blue aster into a meadow rose.

No, all the pushing and accelerating in the world won't turn an aster into a rose. And pushing any child to perform a task for which they are not developmentally prepared is an exercise in futility, perhaps abusive futility.

To illustrate that simple point, consider walking. If you were to survey a group of 100 parents in any setting anywhere in the world and ask, "At what age did your child take her first unaided walking steps?" the responses would be the same. A few would say "at 9 months," a few more "at 10 months." The answers would eventually form a perfectly symmetrical bell curve representing the variation in this aspect of child development. The peak of the curve would be around 12 or 13 months, with responses thinning out at and beyond 15 months. I suspect you are not shocked.

Now imagine anxious parents repeatedly pulling their one-year-old from the sidewalk, knees bleeding, and insisting "Walk, damn it!!!" Or, to torture the analogy (rather than the child), imagine hiring an expensive walking tutor because your child did not get out of her bed and walk across the room on her first birthday. It's nonsense, of course, but this is precisely what we are doing to children every day in American schools and homes, when pressing them to do "academic" tasks for which they are not ready.

Fifteen years ago I had a short, fascinating exchange with Jerome Bruner, whom I mentioned in Chapter 2 in my short summary of progressive education's roots. Bruner, who died with too little notice in June 2016, influenced my own thinking about children and education, long before I became a Head of School. Having encountered something (now forgotten) that evoked my affection for Bruner's work, I Googled him and discovered to my surprise that he was still active, serving in an emeritus position at New York University, as he was until his death. I found his email address and posed a question, not really expecting a reply. To my surprise, he replied within a day or two.

I can't recall my question, but I'll never forget his answer. The latter had nothing to do with the former. Evidently provoked by my self-identification as head of a school, he proceeded to tell me exactly what he thought ailed education in America. He was referring explicitly to supposedly "good" schools, private like Calhoun, or public schools in more advantaged communities – he understood that the problems in less privileged communities are primarily problems of poverty and despair, not educational philosophy. I wish I had saved the email, but I can confidently characterize its contents.

He wrote that the greatest flaw in our approach to children and learning is the impulse to expect students to do too much too soon. This admonition, while always important, should be more urgently heeded in the current frenetic push to infuse early childhood education with pre-academic or academic work.

The problems are two-fold.

First, Bruner declared, the pressure of academic work on young children will inevitably lead to great frustration. This frustration can have devastating cognitive and psychological consequences. Among them is to make learning and school unpleasant for children. Short-term unpleasantness is bad enough, because it can quickly lead to a lifetime aversion to any school environment. Of even greater significance is that frustration is accompanied by elevation of cortisol levels in the brain. Both fear and frustration – companion emotions when children are in the presence of stern teachers with "high expectations" – drive cortisol levels higher. And high levels of cortisol inhibit learning. Another key hormone, dopamine, is critical because it facilitates motivation and learning, yet stress depletes dopamine. As I will address in another context later, these simple scientific realities makes "high stakes testing" a rather odd educational policy, yet it is the dominant policy imperative of the last 20 or 30 years. That is, quite literally, crazy.

But Bruner's second point is more important and less obvious. He wrote that a collateral effect of pressing children to do early academic work is to reward conformity – a particularly damaging kind of conformity. When confronted with the demands of academic work, young children rapidly determine that learning consists of pleasing the authoritative adult in the learning environment. This is true at home as well as school. Young children, having no significant capacity for critical or abstract thought, will want to find the "right" answer whenever questioned by a teacher, parent or caregiver. Providing the desired response, even if only by trial and error, will draw positive reinforcement. Receiving praise or affirmation from a powerful adult is a near-aphrodisiac to a child. While Bruner is not specifically a behaviorist, this conditioning over time has a major effect on children. School becomes a place where getting answers "right," in the estimable opinion of the teacher, is the only thing that really matters. Other cognitive and psychological behaviors are weakened or extinguished in the service of praise seeking.

This phenomenon is of paramount importance in understanding the shortcomings, often debilitating, of rigorous conventional education. At the privileged end of the continuum, it produces incurious grade-grubbers like my young friend's Princeton classmates I described in Chapter 2. At the other end of the spectrum, this expectation of conformity extinguishes imagination, represses curiosity, and is stealing childhood from a generation of poor children.

Despite Bruner's clear warnings, the press of early academic work has accelerated in recent years. Reading, in particular, is a topic of near constant angst in and out of schools. Properly seen as critical currency for a successful life, literacy is the most hotly debated issue in school and curriculum design. Offering reading instruction to young children is not the answer, despite what might be good intentions. Academic work for small children is both a sin of commission and a sin of omission. The sin of commission is, as Bruner argues, that children are not developmentally ready for instruction, and it is likely to make school stressful for them. It also doesn't work.

The pseudo-scientific educational rhetoric around early learning is offensively arcane. An article in *Education Evaluation and Policy Analysis* is a case in point. It states:

Duration and dosage effects of ECE

The influence of program duration on children's outcomes is essential for understanding whether two years of Head Start would be more beneficial for children than one year of Head Start followed by one year of pre-k. [48]

"Dosage effects?!" This is how education experts talk about children? Well, not all experts.

In the wonderful book, *A Mandate for Playful Learning in Preschool: Presenting the Evidence,* [49] Kathy Hirsh-Pasek, Roberta Golinkoff and colleagues argue convincingly that placing children in a setting too advanced for their developmental (not chronological) age may actually delay or inhibit their mastery of reading and comprehension. Pressing children quite likely will create children and adults who consider reading a chore rather than a joy. But despite all of this, we do it anyway. Similarly compelling evidence is provided in other books, including *Endangered Minds: Why Children Don't Think And What We Can Do About It,* [39] by Jane M. Healy (grandparent to a former Calhoun student) and *Wounded by School: Recaptur-*

ing the Joy in Learning and Standing Up to Old School Culture,
[50] by Kirsten Olson.

The sin of omission may be even more harmful. Stretching from progressive education's earliest roots to the books cited above (and dozens more), the evidence is unambiguous – early childhood education should be play-based and social. Pre-school and kindergarten are the years when children are developing social skills and learning to be members of a community, albeit a rather small one. Pre-school and kindergarten are not the time for "dosing" with pre-academic medicine. Early childhood programs that require children to sit still or do school work are depriving them of the social and neurobiological experiences that are the very foundation of later cognitive and social development.

The value of pre-school rests in its lack of highly structured intentions. 3 and 4-year old children have such widely varied developmental timelines that a standard curriculum is nonsensical. The evidence for the importance of play is unambiguous, and the play should be imaginative and open-ended, not teacher-directed and pre-academic.

The irony is that the children who least need pre-school in America are the ones for whom it is readily available. Privileged children have the luxury of play-based, developmentally flexible pre-schools like the one at my school. I'm not suggesting that it has no value, but most of Calhoun's pre-school students might do just fine without our program. Many, not all, of our pre-school parents also have time to arrange play dates, play groups, or other social activities. These families also have homes rich in print and oral language and engaging toys for their toddlers to freely explore. For these folks, pre-school is a lovely extension of a set of advantages that accompany privilege. It is also a way for kids to have these experiences while parents pursue satisfying work.

In less privileged communities, families don't have these advantages. For them, the need for pre-school is inarguably greater. Without pre-school, these children are too likely to remain in environments where oral and print language is less abundant, where resources don't allow for creative toys, and where parents are too overwhelmed by just making ends meet.

So it's hard to object to the advent of "universal pre-school," because the intent is laudatory. Unfortunately, as is the case with highly regimented charter schools and urban public schools, public pre-schools are being designed for children in less privileged communities. The last thing we need is for the standards and accountability crowd to design pre-school programs. I can only imagine that Pearson is already designing materials for the new pre-school market, and technology entrepreneurs are drooling over the possibility of online pre-school. Play groups on Skype!! Imagine the scalability!

Education reform, including this movement for universal pre-school, is accompanied by insistence on strict accountability. Severe accountability is always directed toward the goose and seldom the gander. It reminds me of a proposal in New Hampshire a few years back that would have required that food stamp recipients be drug-tested. When we grant subsidies to large corporations, or bailed out the financial institutions that led our economy to the brink, we don't ask their leaders to take semi-annual drug tests. But we always insist that the least advantaged among us provide proof that our precious dollars are being spent with measurable efficacy. When it comes to providing a decent early childhood experience for all young children can't we just be generous of spirit?

Natural Development and Reading

When considering the importance of natural development and the wrongheadedness of early academic work, reading is perhaps the most misunderstood aspect of schools. Reading is an invaluable skill and the emphasis on reading and reading readiness is understandable. But a conventional, rigorous approach in early childhood is neither necessary nor useful.

Whether through the older lenses of Vygotsky, Piaget, Bruner et al, or through the more current neurobiological research, the brain maturation that allows reading to take hold is varied. Any teacher knows that some children will begin to read (or appear to begin to read) by age 4 or 5, while others will not do so until age 7, 8 or later.

It doesn't matter. Early readers are not better readers, or better students, or better people. Delays in reading may be but are rarely related to a learning anomaly, but patience is the first line of intervention. Parents or teachers who expect all 6 or 7 year-olds to begin reading are as unrealistic (and perhaps as cruel) as the hypothetical parent saying "walk, damn it" to his 12 month-old daughter. Not only is the anxiety fruitless – it sets in motion a complex set of emotional reactions to learning, school, teachers and parents that may take a lifetime to fully overcome. All for nothing.

Many other nations, the much-touted Finland as one example, don't teach reading until age 7. Other schools in Europe wait until 8. Abundant evidence shows that these students read just as well or better than children who began reading instruction at much earlier ages. So what's the hurry?

Sebastian Suggate, a researcher at the University of Otago in New Zealand, has done extensive research. Suggate examined data from 54 countries and found "no association between school entry age ... and reading achievement at age 15." As with my affection for Wendy Mogel's wildflower metaphor, I particularly enjoy how Suggate describes the effects of premature reading instruction:

> *(It is like) watering a garden before a rainstorm; the earlier watering is rendered undetectable by the rainstorm, the watering wastes precious water, and the watering detracts the gardener from other important preparatory groundwork.* [51]

Although it is admittedly at the extreme, one Calhoun student, whose grandmother was Calhoun's long time Lower School Director, didn't read fluently until age 11 or 12. She, and the boy's mother, refused to have him "remediated." He received a $30,000 writing scholarship to college several years later.

One of the most compelling critics of the mechanized, early approach to reading is Canadian Frank Smith, a proponent of what is called "whole language." Among his many books, *Unspeakable Acts, Unnatural Practices: Flaws and Fallacies in Scientific Reading Instruction* [52] provides a powerful argument for a progressive, naturalistic approach to reading (and all other learning). The partners Ken and Yetta Goodman, both Emeriti Professors at the University of Arizona, are notable among many others, including linguist and activist Noam Chomsky, who have advanced the whole language cause. They are following the earlier theoretical path walked by Dewey, Vygotsky, Bruner and others. The intellectual heft of this approach to reading and learning is considerable, yet schools continue to engage in the unspeakable acts and unnatural practices that Smith debunked.

I don't suggest that early experience is irrelevant. There is little doubt that a rich language environment is an important precondition to literacy. Reading to children, having books and large letters to view at home and in school, and having real conversations with toddlers are all important parts of a foundation for literacy.

A widely publicized study from 1995, [53] conducted by University of Kansas psychologists Betty Hart and Todd R. Risley, introduced the idea of a 30 million-word advantage enjoyed by children in privileged communities. By pre-school age they had been exposed to nearly triple the number of spoken words as less privileged peers. Kathy Hirsh-Pasek, to whom I referred earlier, is among several researchers cited in a 2014 article in *The New York Times* [54] indicating that the number of words was actually not the critical variable. It was the conversational context of the language, especially between and among family members, which mattered. This is another affirmation of the work of Bruner and others I've cited who all understood the importance of learning written language in social context.

The language deficit experienced by children who live in poverty can be near crippling, but the answer is not phonics instruction in pre-school. The answer lies in addressing poverty, providing jobs and livable wages for parents, helping to keep families and communities intact, and offering good health care (including pre-natal education for parents), all of which will contribute to giving children the foundation needed for learning.

Again, to emphasize the prescience of progressive educators, contemporary understanding of natural development in reading flows from a clear chronological progression of learning theory – Piaget influenced Vygotsky, who influenced Bruner, Chomsky, the Goodmans and others.

Much attention is given to research that purports to demonstrate that late readers fall further behind in school with each passing year. Therefore our national policy has been to insure that every 3rd grader is a fluent reader – as though a national policy can actually change the reality of children! While it is true that a late reader may have subsequent difficulty in school, this is not because of some intrinsic problem with delayed reading, it is because subsequent curriculum has reading by 3rd grade as a prerequisite. Kids who can't read well by 3rd grade will become increasing frustrated and alienated, they will internalize the idea that they are stupid, and will increasingly fulfill that sad prophecy.

Natural Development and Mathematics

This range of developmental readiness applies to all aspects of cognitive development, including the other Holy Grail of achievement – mathematics. From the earliest steps – counting objects – to the later abstractions, the age at which children "get it," varies significantly within a broad and normal range on the continuum of development. Here too, precocious learners are not necessarily more brilliant adult mathematicians. It is a matter of individual development, not comprehensive intelligence. This continues far beyond early childhood.

I recall an angry parent chastising a middle school math teacher because his child wasn't "getting" long division in 5th grade. The teacher, to my delight, said, "Why are you so angry and worried? Some kids get it in 5th grade, some don't, but I've never had an 8th grader who couldn't do long division." As with late readers, some slower developers go on to excel in advanced calculus and major in math or science in college, unless they are serially humiliated as a consequence of their natural developmental timeline.

Here too, there is powerful evidence of the advantages of a more patient approach. In the 1930's, Louis P. Benezet, superintendent of the Manchester, New Hampshire school district, believed that excessive math instruction was "dulling and almost chloroforming" children's reasoning abilities. He had observed that the children in Manchester schools were not good at solving novel mathematics problems and that the time devoted to rote arithmetic work was also detracting from students' enjoyment of reading, writing and oral expression.

He designed a large-scale experiment [55] using the entire district. It is important to note that the experimental group was comprised of schools in the less wealthy neighborhoods of Manchester. He rightly worried that the more-privileged parents would object to the experiment. He thereby also, perhaps unintentionally, insured that those who might claim the outcome was due to the advantages the wealthier children enjoyed could not discredit the results.

In the experimental schools he banned the formal teaching of arithmetic before 6th grade. Instead:

The children in these rooms were encouraged to do a great deal of oral composition. They reported on books that they had read, on incidents which they had seen, on visits that they had made. They told the stories of movies that they had attended and they made up romances on the spur of the moment. [55]

Mathematics was not banned entirely, but it was to be approached only in experiential contexts, for example when the school day presented an opportunity to measure things or estimate the height of a tree. No formal math classes were permitted. The control group schools (remember, in the more advantaged neighborhoods) were to continue with the math intensive curriculum, several hours a day, as it had been taught. Business as usual. This split in curriculum and practice continued through 3rd, 4th and 5th grades. As they entered 6th grade, all students moved into the same 6th grade math curriculum, implemented in the conventional way, precisely as was the case prior to the study.

The outcomes are astonishing to those who think "earlier" and "more" are the way to improve academic achievement. As expected, the experimental students who were "encouraged to do a great deal of oral composition" were significantly more developed in their use and understanding of language by 6th grade.

As Benezet expected, the experimental students were slightly behind their control group peers in math at the beginning of 6th grade. After all, they had never encountered some of the work they were expected to do. But, as he had hypothesized, the deficit was erased in a few months, with no additional instruction required. His claim that the lack of formal training did not inhibit their mathematical performance was validated.

More important, he tested both groups with an abstract

mathematical puzzle. None of the students in the control group, who had spent thousands of hours on arithmetic studies during the prior years, were able to solve the puzzle. All of the students in the experimental group, who had learned math only in experiential context – playing, measuring, building, estimating – were able to solve the puzzle very quickly. While this was not a formal part of his experimental model, the results – "none" in the control group and "all" in the experimental group – are, to say the least, statistically significant.

Benezet's remarkable experiment, known to very few educators, not only demonstrated that patience did no harm. He demonstrated that patience and a more progressive approach to mathematical ideas actually produced more capable students.

Consequences of Unnatural Practices and Environments

The failure of educational policy and practice to acknowledge and respond patiently to the natural and varied developmental trajectories of children has spawned several very damaging industries.

The first industry, which plagues schools across the privilege continuum, is tutoring and remediation. I am skeptical of the burgeoning field of learning disabilities or, more euphemistically, learning differences. This is not to suggest that dyslexia or other brain differences are mythological. While working as an administrator at Landmark College in Vermont, a school dedicated to serving college-age students with learning issues, I knew students with profound, brain-based challenges who had been dismally neglected by previous schools. But I have also seen scores of expensive educational assessments, filled with pseudo-intellectual, arcane language that makes perfectly normal children seem profoundly disabled.

Several decades ago a very prestigious Manhattan private school was given a large donation to have all their students assessed. A great many were "diagnosed" with some kind of learning disability. As you might imagine, a PR problem erupted within the school community when parents paying high tuition learned that their children were flawed. Of course the assessments were nonsense, and they simply identified the various ways that each child strayed from some theoretical norm. In 1994 *The New York Times* reported as follows: [56]

[The school's] new team of remedial specialists suddenly began finding enormous numbers of bright little children with learning problems. In one three-year period, 77 of 215 [of the school's] 5-year-olds (36 percent) were labeled "at risk" during their second month of kindergarten and given remedial help. That is far higher than the national rate for learning problems. These were kindergartners with a mean I.Q. of 132, at a school that traditionally sends 40 percent of its seniors to Ivy League colleges.

Parents who just a few months earlier had been proud to have a 5-year-old accepted to [the school] and elated about the youngster's I.Q. score were suddenly being told that a new Fisher Landau screening test indicated "potential visual motor problems" or "sequencing ability deficits."

A learning disability industry grew at [the school]. Instead of being comforted by the school's remedial help, many parents were unnerved and sought even more tutoring and therapy for their children after school from private *specialists at a rate of $75 to $200 an hour, said the former school psychologist.*

By 1992, half of [the school's] students entering 4th grade had already received remedial help. Several [of the school's] teachers describe their classrooms as being overrun by specialists. One teacher, who had half her class diagnosed with learning problems, says she simply gave up arguing with the specialists and used the Fisher Landau program for her entire class.

I'd like to report that this experience was instructive and that private schools have come to their senses, but this phenomenon is still rampant, at least in Manhattan.

This rush to label, intervene and remediate is particularly pervasive around reading. Anecdotal reports suggest that the majority of kids in some private schools are being tutored, to "catch up," or, equally foolishly, to "get ahead." A waste of time and money to be sure, but also guaranteed to affect a child's sense of self. I offered this advice to Calhoun parents several years ago:

Even in New York City's unique culture, where it sometimes seems that all adults have therapists and all children have tutors, tutoring has consequences that should be seriously contemplated. As every hour of tutoring is also an hour not doing something else, tutoring is an act of omission: Omitting play dates and their crucial social development role in a child's life; Omitting fun family activity; Omitting outdoor time; Omitting day dreaming and fantastic play.

The child may infer any number of things from tutoring

sessions: *"I'm not very smart." "My parents don't think I'm very smart." "I can't learn things very well without help." "My parents are really worried about me."* In a few instances parents have told me that their child really, really likes going to the tutor. Perhaps. Children like to please their parents and some tutors really make things fun. It's much more likely that the child is compliant than that the child is happy. Children depend on us to make the right choices for them. They are not equipped to make the argument that tutoring is unnecessary. Or are they?

While wishing to protect the specific individuals, I share a story from one of Calhoun's best, most experienced teachers. She recently spent time with a Lower School student who is being tutored regularly, despite our assessment that she is making appropriate progress.

The child reported that the tutor said that she was "reading below grade level compared to kids from other schools." Boo to the tutor.

The child told the tutor, "But we are all different and we go to different schools." Brava to the child.

The tutor says, "The books you read are too easy." Boo to the tutor.

The child says, "But I feel these books are good for me." Brava to the child.

At this point the child showed the Calhoun teacher the book she was reading, desperately hoping for approval, which the teacher offered with affection and conviction. She asked the child if she had talked to her parents about her feeling that tutoring wasn't needed.

Her reply? "Grownups always believe other grownups, so I don't think they will believe me."

Finally, tutoring can create unnecessary conflict with the school. If we de-emphasize a particularly activity (repetitious and stressful spelling and vocabulary tests in Lower School, for example) for important cognitive and emotional reasons, what is conveyed to the child by engaging in tutoring that emphasizes precisely those things? If the school takes a flexible, innovative approach to early mathematics, what conflict arises when a tutor has a very rote, traditional approach to mathematics? There are instances where the heavily tutored child simply shuts down in school – afraid to participate, fatigued from hours of "concentration."

There is little question that the time and money spent on tutoring will often produce a measurable result in performance on the tasks being tutored, but at what cost and for what purpose? There is a counterintuitive argument, supported by intriguing evidence, that repetitive tutoring on specific tasks actually inhibits long-term intellectual development. Proving this may be challenging, but it is as or more convincing than any evidence that early tutoring produces later intellectual brilliance.

Having reviewed hundreds of reports and observed thousands of children, I am skeptical about claims of progress due to tutoring. The reports often show that tutored students make progress. I suggest that the progress is not necessarily caused by the tutoring, but may be a result of the developmental changes that occur over the time span of tutoring.

To return to the walking analogy, if an anxious parent of a

one year-old non-walker hires a walking tutor, at some point the child will actually stand up and walk. The tutor was an irrelevant, and costly, variable.

I attribute this to what's known in psychology as superstitious behavior. An example of superstitious behavior – chickens in cages were studied to assess the effects of reinforcement schemes on their behavior. Reinforcement came in the form of a food pellet dropped down a small slide. The experimenter could reinforce a particular behavior in various ways – every time the behavior was exhibited or at intermittent incidences of the behavior. If, for example, they wanted to strengthen cackling, they would reward the chicken when it cackled, either every time or on some intermittent basis. Among the findings, as behaviorists might expect, is that the intermittent rewards actually strengthened learning more than the "per response" rewards did.

But the surprise finding was that every once in a while, when random food service was provided to control group chickens, a very strange thing happened. Remember, the rewards were programmed to be completely random, unrelated to any behavior. A chicken might, for example, happen to turn clockwise when a pellet dropped. No big deal. Then, by chance, the chicken turned a bit further in a clockwise direction and another pellet dropped. If this happened a few times, the chicken would infer a cause and effect relationship and begin turning clockwise intentionally. If the chicken persisted in the behavior long enough, another pellet would inevitably arrive. The interval between pellets didn't matter. This accidental conditioning led some chickens to literally whirl like dervishes, believing their frenetic, ever-faster turning was the cause of the reward. Some spun themselves to death. This is superstitious behavior.

And, as you probably might expect, superstitious behavior is a major contributor to the industrial tutoring/school complex. Most students who are tutored, at rates up to $500/hour, do sometimes improve on the tasks for which they are being tutored, but it is likely they would have improved anyway even without the tutoring. This might be viewed as a benign form of income redistribution, since few tutors are as wealthy as the families who hire them, but the process itself is not benign. The tutored children are losing valuable hours when they could be daydreaming or playing with friends – activities which would have far greater cognitive value than tutoring.

The other industry is more harmful – the diagnostic epidemic of Attention Deficit Hyperactivity Disorder (ADHD) and its diminutive sibling ADD.

In October 2014, Dr. Richard A. Friedman, a Professor of Clinical Psychiatry and Director of the Psychopharmacology Clinic at Weill Cornell Medical College, wrote an Op-Ed piece for *The New York Times.* [57] He offered the alarming statistic that 11% of children between ages 4 and 17 suffer at some time from this "disorder." Since then the use of medications has exploded, increasing 28% in four years. Perhaps most alarming was his report that some 10,000 toddlers, aged 2 and 3, were being medicated. Friedman concluded his article with the following comment:

> *In school, these curious, experience-seeking kids would most likely do better in small classes that emphasize hands-on-learning, self-paced computer assignments and tasks that build specific skills. This will not eliminate the need for many kids with A.D.H.D. to take psychostimulants. But let's not rush to medicalize their curiosity,*

energy and novelty-seeking; in the right environment, these traits are not a disability, and can be a real asset.

Perhaps the most disturbing aspect of the research regarding medical intervention is the flawed assumptions our system holds about standardized tests. This research assumes that sitting still for a standardized test is an important measure of ability. But making a young girl or boy sit still to take a standardized test is, as Frank Smith might say, an unspeakable act and unnatural practice in and of itself. Therefore what the research really indicates is that we should medicate young children so that they are better able to perform unnatural acts.

Sadly, "high stakes" standardized tests are unlikely to be going away soon. Some children are able to survive the stress and perform unnatural acts without resorting to the unspeakable assault of medication. But for families blessed with children who have so-called attention problems, it is a Faustian bargain. If you risk the known and unknown effects of medication and go against your parental instincts, your child may do better on these meaningless tests, which nonetheless have high stakes despite their low meaning. I don't minimize the difficulty of the choice and I don't blame parents who choose medication.

Betsy Hoza, a psychology professor at the University of Vermont, has demonstrated improvement from exercise in impulse control and focus among children aged 5-8 who have been diagnosed with ADHD. [58]

This research reveals deep irony, as children with ADHD are often removed from recess or other physical activities, simply because of impulsive behavior that would actually benefit from the physical activity they are being denied! Unspeakable, unnatural and stupid.

The good news is that the mechanism that triggers improvement from either medication or exercise may be very much the same. Each increases brain levels of dopamine and norepinephrine, both of which are thought to aid in concentration and impulse control.

The following are some of the side effects of Ritalin and other similar medications used to treat ADHD: [59]

Common Side Effects

- Addiction

- Nervousness including agitation, anxiety and irritability

- Trouble sleeping (insomnia)

- Decreased appetite

- Headache

- Stomach ache

- Nausea

- Dizziness

- Heart palpitations

Other Serious Side Effects Include

- Slowing of growth (height and weight) in children

- Seizures, mainly in patients with a history of seizures

- Eyesight changes or blurred vision

Less Common Side Effects

- Tolerance (constant need to raise the dose)

- Feelings of suspicion and paranoia

- Visual hallucinations (seeing things that are not there)

- Depression

- Cocaine craving

In contrast, exercise has these beneficial side effects – it lowers the incidence of obesity, prevents diabetes, prevents cardiovascular disease, strengthens bones and connective tissue, and is fun! And many, many more.

Which side effects would you choose for your child?

The best solution for all children, but especially those diagnosed with ADHD, is to avoid standardized tests and all other unnatural educational practices. But if unnatural educational practices are inevitable, families should at least be able to avoid the unspeakable act of medicating their very young children. Exercise is certainly a viable alternative, if only schools would encourage it.

Friedman points out that ADHD is a relatively recent human "disorder." ADHD likely became elevated to a pathology only when its attributes stopped being useful. Regimented, demanding school environments don't reward the adventure-seeking, stimulus-craving traits of such children. In an earlier time the traits of ADHD were an evolutionary advantage, as curiosity, high energy, and an appetite for adventure were assets in activities like exploration and hunting.

Friedman also reported that many ADHD children grow out of the disorder, making the epidemic of diagnosis and medication treatment among young children even more troubling.

The over-medication of children is a product of a combustible duo – the greed of the pharmaceutical industry and unnatural school environments. As Jerome Bruner wrote in 1987, "If you construct a classroom in which children must keep their seats, you are assuring that there will be a hyperactivity syndrome." Rather than design schools that respond to the wonderful, boisterous, energetic reality of children, we medicate children so that they will conform to the unnatural design and expectations of rigid, inhumane schools. It is a national shame.

I'm not much on parables, but this one from Zorba the Greek is beautiful and apt:

> *I remembered one morning when I discovered a cocoon in the bark of a tree, just as a butterfly was making a hole in its case and preparing to come out. I waited a while, but it was too long appearing and I was impatient. I bent over and breathed on it to warm it. I warmed it as quickly as I could and the miracle began to happen before my eyes, faster than life. The case opened, the butterfly started crawling out and I shall never forget my horror when I saw how its wings were folded back and crumpled; the wretched butterfly tried with its whole trembling body to unfold them. Bending over it, I tried to help it with my breath, in vain.*

> *It needed to be hatched out patiently and the unfolding of the wings should be a gradual process in the sun. Now it was too late. My breath had forced the butterfly to appear, all crumpled, before its time. It struggled desperately and, a few seconds later, died in the palm of my hand. That little body is, I do believe, the greatest weight I have on my conscience. For I realize today that it is a mortal sin*

to violate the great laws of nature. We should not hurry, we should not be impatient, but we should confidently obey the eternal rhythm.

Remember this when someone suggests a little more rigor, tutoring, or medication in a young child's education.

Chapter Five

Motivation

A contemporary understanding of extrinsic and intrinsic motivation provides essential affirmation of the advantages of progressive education. "Extrinsic" and "intrinsic" motivational systems are likely to be familiar notions, particularly to educators, but a brief definition may be helpful.

Extrinsic motivation, especially in education, is driven by systems of rewards and punishments. Although rewards and punishments seem like opposite forces, in this respect they are simply two sides of the same coin. "Ex," indicates "out of," thereby "extrinsic" means those things that are "out of" an individual. Obvious examples are grades, gold stars, M&M's, lavish parental praise, pay bonuses, and so on. Someone other than the individual in question has their hand on the levers of reward. The flip side, punishment, may be the withholding of these things, or it may be more explicit punishment such as an "F," grade, suspension from school, shunning, expulsion, early bedtime, no television, or spanking. Again, with extrinsic motivation, the consequences of one's actions are externally determined.

Intrinsic motivation is driven by factors that emanate from within, such as self-satisfaction, desire for mastery, curiosity, fulfillment, pleasure, self-realization, desire for independence, ethical needs, etc. Intrinsic motivation is a powerful innate characteristic of all human beings, across all cultures and societies.

For purposes of examining "extrinsic" and "intrinsic" motivation in an education context I refer specifically to the work of Mark R. Lepper, Sheena Sethi, Dania Dialdin and Michael Drake. Their 1997 article, "Intrinsic and Extrinsic Motivation: A Developmental Perspective" [60] is a fine summary of the research into the relationship between extrinsic and intrinsic and the effect on students and schools.

The research they summarize is quite consistent, at least on one point – young children have strong intrinsic motivation to learn. Anyone who spends time with toddlers knows of their insatiable curiosity. This intrinsic drive continues into school, at least for a while. Children continue to be curious and to want to learn all manner of things.

A 2013 TED talk [61] by Sugata Mitra, Professor of Educational Technology at Newcastle University in England, provides evidence of intrinsic motivation among children. He tried an experiment, expecting no particular outcome, placing personal computers in public spaces in his native India, in neighborhoods where children were not well educated. Among other obstacles, the software was in English and the children spoke no English. In response to questions like "what should we do?" he was good humored and non-committal. "Whatever you'd like, or nothing at all." Over a period of several weeks the children deciphered the software, learned to type without ever before having seen a keyboard, and did all kinds of other things. Responding to critics who thought perhaps experts helped the children, he repeated this in more remote locations, where the odds against encountering a software designer were astronomical. In one iteration of this rural experiment he loaded a complex piece of college level curriculum about DNA (in English) on the computer for the kids to find, assuming they would ignore it or find it utterly incomprehensible. He reports humorously about an 11 year-old girl soon thereafter describing the association between damaged DNA and disease.

I report this with caution, as it could further encourage rooms full of computers for children as a scalable and cost-effective approach to learning. I do think his experiment supports the premise that children are naturally curious, intrinsically motivated, and more capable than adults might think.

Then something changes. From 3rd grade to 8th or 9th grade there is a steady decline in intrinsic motivation.

The full analysis of extrinsic and intrinsic motivation is complicated. Extrinsic motivation is not entirely bad, since it can encourage students to try novel things. Rewards, within reason, can encourage continued striving. But the overwhelming consensus is that intrinsic motivation is more powerful, lasting and beneficial. Since intrinsic motivation declines, and extrinsic motivation stays the same, overall motivation to learn declines with age. And that's not a good thing. I believe this decline is less likely in progressive schools, for reasons that will be self-evident.

Since intrinsic motivation declines as extrinsic structures dramatically increase, the stakes get higher. Tests increase in frequency and duration. Expectations around college and achievement ratchet up. Grade point averages, honor roles, valedictorians, salutatorians, class ranks, and honor societies – all of these forms of extrinsic motivation are ubiquitous.

Jerome Bruner adds another element to explain the decline of intrinsic motivation. As pointed out earlier, Bruner and progressive theorists describe the importance of learning in context. Bruner in particular defined social relationships and context as a critical variable in language development. John Dewey and countless others argued for the connection between education and real experience, both as a matter of philosophical conviction and pedagogical wisdom.

But, as Bruner points out, learning becomes steadily de-contextualized as children move from grade to grade. As school becomes more controlled, more about instruction than exploration, more about abstraction than experience, children's natural intrinsic motivation declines.

This is, perhaps, a similar explanation for what Lepper et al suggest when reporting, "… declines in intrinsic motivation may be due to the more general social characteristics of schools …" In this regard they also cite the work of Jacquelynne Eccles and Allan Wigfield, [62] who, among other things, have shown the negative effect that "high control" school environments have on intrinsic motivation. Teacher-directed, tightly scripted rote exercises and competition erode intrinsic motivation.

Even those learning activities that were initially driven by intrinsic motivation will weaken after they have been exposed to extrinsic structures. Let's say a student loves reading for intrinsic reasons – curiosity, self-fulfillment and enjoyment. Then the reading activity is incentivized – a treat for reading a book, a gold star on a list in the classroom. Thereafter, the intrinsic motivation for reading grows weaker. This is an extraordinarily important concept to understand in designing school practices, but is apparently unknown to or ignored by a great many educators.

Referring to Lepper et al., Eccles and Wigfield add that "… still other studies have suggested a link between children's extrinsic motivational orientation and their vulnerability to helplessness in the face of failure, and possibly even their susceptibility to depression." [62] This finding is of great importance in analyzing the rising levels of stress, depression and eating disorders among high achieving students, as discussed in Chapter 2.

And this is a powerfully important point. Even as the extrinsic structures in schooling grow nearly exponentially, there is no increase in extrinsic motivation. So why would anyone design or encourage this kind of school program or culture?

Finally, to accentuate the point, this delightful connection to progressive history and practice from the 1997 Lepper article:

Moreover, all of these beneficial effects on motivation and learning can be shown to increase significantly if the concrete context is personalized on the basis of students' interests, backgrounds or specific choices (e.g. Anand and Ross, 1987; Cordova and Lepper, 1996; Ross, 1983).

At a higher level, these same considerations underlie considerably more general calls for the increased use of what has been called the "project approach" to schooling (e.g. Edwards, Gandini, and Forman, 1993; Katz and Chard, 1989) – an idea that dates back at least to John Dewey (1913, 1938). In this model, the goal is to integrate a variety of traditional curriculum goals into the pursuit of long-term projects selected on the basis of students' demonstrated interests. [60]

If we hope that children will continue to strive and be highly motivated to learn, sustaining their innate intrinsic motivation is essential. And this is what progressive education has done since the 18th century, with its emphasis on student choice, student-centered schools and project based learning.

Understanding the importance of intrinsic motivation and the negative aspects of extrinsic structures calls into question a great deal about conventional school practices and educational reform. Despite the complete lack of demonstrable improvement in schools, reformers are doubling down on extrinsic structures, demeaning, degrading and demotivating millions of children and their teachers.

My purpose is not to fully flesh out the research as regards motivation, but to support the central proposition of this book – that progressive education had it right all along. And that case, from a motivational point of view, seems unassailable.

Chapter Six

Multiple Intelligences – Individual Differences

The concept of multiple intelligences is arguably the single most important advance in how we should think about children and learning. Yet we don't. Although admittedly a limited sample, my 17 years of talking with parents of prospective students yields a rather alarming reality. At admission events, when I briefly summarize multiple intelligence theory, I ask those present if they have even heard the phrase or are familiar with the work of Howard Gardner. In a typical audience of 120-150 highly educated New York City parents, only 4 or 5 raise their hands. How can we have a purposeful conversation about schools or educational policy when something this fundamental is not part of common knowledge?

As summarized in Chapter 2, Gardner proposed that our dualistic view of intelligence (linguistic and logical-mathematical) was insufficient. He proposed 5 other ways in which humans are intelligent – musical-rhythmic, visual-spatial, bodily-kinesthetic, interpersonal, and intrapersonal. In later years he proposed that naturalistic and existential intelligence be added to the inventory.

A very brief summary of each intelligence may be helpful in developing an understanding of how and why these descriptors should inform good educational practice. I'll skip linguistic and logical mathematical, as they are the default understanding of intelligence that has dominated educational practice for several centuries.

Musical-rhythmic intelligence is among the more obvious of the remaining seven. The ability to discern pitch, replicate a melody, identify intervals of sound, understand complex rhythms and, in the aggregate, perceive and create interesting and beautiful sounds. Some of us are more "musical" than others and Gardner rightly acknowledges this as intelligence, not just an isolated talent. This is particularly important in language acquisition, as I explicate in a Chapter 7 when discussing the power of the arts in education.

Visual-spatial intelligence might be observed in one who perceives order out of what others see as chaos. An architect is likely to have a high degree of this intelligence, as is an artist, a good puzzle solver, someone who recognizes patterns, and one who easily interprets charts, graphs or other visual forms of data representation.

Interpersonal intelligence is present in the ability to relate well to other people, to function well in a group, to create positive relationships with others and to be skilled at resolving conflict. Such intelligence is often characterized as "people skills" or emotional intelligence. I prefer to think of this intelligence as analogous to the capacity for empathy.

Intrapersonal intelligence is the capacity for introspection, self-awareness, and a likely interest in theories and ideas. Intrapersonal intelligence is similar to meta-cognition – the act of thinking about how one thinks.

Naturalistic intelligence is the ability to observe and understand patterns in the natural environment. This may be apparent in someone who recognizes and classifies species, or sees the patterns in biology or botany.

Existential intelligence involves an individual's ability to intuitively understand social groups, meaning in life, systems of ethics or philosophical theories, and other complex matters that require a "big picture" view of existence.

I saved **bodily-kinesthetic intelligence** for last because it is the most counter-intuitive. We usually describe folks with abundant bodily-kinesthetic intelligence as good athletes. When talking about multiple intelligences to those who are unfamiliar with the concept, I use this example:

Imagine a great basketball player taking an in-bounds pass and beginning a journey down the court. The player has already, subconsciously, calculated the precise pressure in the game ball on that day, in that arena, as well as any unusual characteristics of the gym floor. Then she begins to dribble, choosing a precise direction and amount of force with which to propel the ball toward the floor. She may put a small amount of rotation on the sphere during release. She predicts precisely where the ball will rebound so that she might have a hand ready to receive it. She does this repeatedly, with either hand, sometimes behind her back or between her legs. The first few dribbles, with all these variables, would be very challenging to program on a computer. But that's not all. She is also observing 9 other players, their positions on the court, their rates and direction of movement, so that she might avoid them in the trip down the court. At the end of the journey she approaches the basket, spins the ball off the backboard dropping it neatly through the net.

Everything described is based in the brain and is clearly intelligence, not athleticism. It certainly helps to be tall and have a great vertical leap – but this is intelligence just as certainly as is an 800 score on the math section of the SAT.

Gardner is not the only theorist to propose that humans are intelligent in ways other than linguistic and mathematical. To some extent it is intuitive, as we all know people who have abilities that fall outside these realms. But prior to Gardner's more formal explication, these other qualities were seen as talents, traits, or personality characteristics. With the partial exception of musical and visual-spatial, these other ways of intelligence were not seen as worthy of a place in any curriculum. And now, sadly, even music and visual art have been eliminated or moved even further to the periphery of educational practice.

Gardner's work on multiple intelligences should have changed education. But, by and large, it did not. In 1993 he wrote:

As I see it, American education is at a turning point. There are considerable pressures to move very sharply in the direction of 'uniform schooling'; there is also the possibility that our educational system can embrace 'individual-

centered schooling.' A struggle is underway at this moment about the probable direction in which the schools will veer. My own analysis of the scientific evidence indicates that we should as a polity move in the direction of individual-centered schooling. In what follows I indicate why and how such an education might be achieved.

At present the vocal contributors to the debate are calling for 'uniform' schools. Stripped to its essentials, their argument goes as follows. There is a basic set of competences, and a core body of knowledge, which every individual in our society should master. Some individuals are more able than others, and are expected to master this knowledge more rapidly. Schools should be set up in such a way to ensure that the most gifted can move to the top and that the greatest number of individuals will achieve basic knowledge as efficiently as possible. For that reason, there should be the same curriculum for all students, and the same 'standardized' methods of assessment. Students, teachers, administrators, school districts, states, and even the whole nation should be judged in terms of the efficiency and effectiveness with which these common standards are achieved. Paying attention to individual differences is at best a luxury, at worst a deviation from essential educational priorities. [9]

He went on to observe:

Yet I am equally convinced that many of the cures suggested by neoconservative reformers are worse that the disease; and that in any case the proposed cures will not heal the patients. My fundamental quarrel with the uniform comes with my conviction that it is based on a fundamentally flawed view of human cognition – one that I call 'IQ-style thinking' [9]

Gardner's rejection of "IQ-style thinking" was, albeit 90 years too late, a full repudiation of the work of E. L. Thorndike, who was prominent among those who inspired the early 20th century turn from progressive to factory education. Gardner surely was prescient in noting this more contemporary turning point. Too bad we didn't pay better attention. We turned the wrong way a few decades ago, and since then we have driven education over a cliff.

This is not primarily a political book, but this more recent turn away from several hundred years of progressive evolution is both ineffective and scandalous. Perhaps the first extended skirmish in this most recent war was focused on reading. The whole language vs. phonics debate was the subject of federal commissions, scholarly treatises, political vitriol and legislation.

As an educator, I propose that the entire argument was nonsensical. Reading is not entirely one or the other. Printed language is indeed the symbols taken individually and in groups (syllables, words). It is also the concept or idea of the word or phrase that is nestled in the symbolic representation. Learning to pronounce the symbolic representation, using phonetics, is one avenue to understanding the code. One can then extrapolate to the understanding of meaning. Taking the "gestalt" of the symbols and understanding its meaning can also lead one to extrapolate backwards, if you will, and see and hear the underlying phonetic breakdown. Any good teacher knows that this is a "both/and" not an "either/or" proposition.

But that's a digression. The more germane point is that phonics won the day, and still rules the roost for political and business, not educational, reasons. I recommend Denny Taylor's superb book, *Beginning to Read and the Spin Doctors of Science.* [63] Taylor is a grandparent of a current Calhoun student (and the CEO of this book's publishing company). She falls clearly on the whole language side of the debate, but more importantly she exposes the politics and money – big money – behind the phonics-first policy initiatives. One hilarious section describes then-Texas Governor George W. Bush's complicity in the wholesale sale of a chunk of America's educational system.

From a policy point of view it has been downhill ever since. In 2001 No Child Left Behind (NCLB) was a legislative manifestation of the "uniform" approach Gardner warned against. NCLB has been an unmitigated disaster. As I write, we are well past the year (2014) by which time that legislation was supposed to have fixed everything. How's that working out? Partly as a result of this legislation, millions of children are even further behind.

In the wake of this policy debacle, government's educational reformers, led by the non-educator Education Secretary Arne Duncan, "rebranded" the same approach and called it Race to the Top (RTTP). That new "brand," also having had no discernable positive effect on anything, was followed by the Common Core, which is uniform education played out on a grand scale. Then, President Obama signed the Every Student Succeeds Act (ESSA) on December 10, 2015. This act also focuses on accountability and standardization, not on children and learning.

When Gardner warned against the adherence to IQ-style education he worried that other forms of developing intellect and "character" would be shortchanged. I enclosed "character" in quotes, because character education is a common feature of very conventional schools and doesn't really reflect what I, and I suspect Gardner, mean by character. In many schools, character education is a slightly more elaborate version of the Boy Scouts or Sunday School. The development of character in this iteration is just another dimension of uniform education – reciting homilies, odes to old-fashioned virtue, memorizing Scripture or signing an Honor Code. In a later chapter I'll offer a different idea of character education and cite the ways multiple intelligences are central to the development of character in a progressive context.

Part of the argument flowing from an understanding of multiple intelligences is that the realms of life that are created and perceived as a result of these other intelligences are as or more important than linguistic and mathematical developments. These things should be at the center of a school's purpose, not on the fringes.

Great buildings, profound works of visual art, beautiful symphonies, ethical systems, social movements, breathtaking athletic achievements, Otis Redding, scientific discoveries and more are the product of intelligences other than linguistic or logical-mathematical. What Charles Darwin observed in nature was not an algebraic algorithm. Michelangelo, as another example, showed no interest in conventional schooling.

Gardner and progressive educators for centuries knew that attending to all these dimensions of individual children would allow for the richest, deepest learning, to the great benefit of the children and of society. That schools have narrowed education to a sterile training of only linguistic and logical-mathematical intelligence is tragic.

But that's not the only sin of this ignorance. Attending to

multiple intelligences also facilitates a deeper understanding of conventional subjects like reading, writing and arithmetic.

It is not my intent to broadly explicate the neurobiology of learning, but it is accurate to say that the idea of multiple intelligences corresponds quite well to the rapidly increasing body of knowledge about the brain. While Gardner's intelligences are described individually, they are quite interrelated and overlapping. This is analogous to the regions and systems of the brain, where the specificity of function by region or system is often clear, but the apprehension, understanding and functions of ideas and skills are often assembled from coalitions of neural systems between and among areas in the brain.

When learning is considered from a neurobiological point of view, it is important to understand how the brain processes and stores sensory information. All of the senses involved in learning and assembling the information carried in these various stimuli are essential to deep understanding. Progressive educators have known this for many, many years, as represented by the progressive notions of handwork, "learning by doing," experiential education, and so on.

In *Multiple Intelligences, The Theory in Practice,* [9] Gardner describes "The Spectrum Battery," a method of assessment of abilities developed as part of Harvard Project Zero. This system was designed to capture the ways in which children are intelligent that are not captured by IQ tests or through other assessment instruments.

As expected, The Spectrum Battery revealed what Gardner's theory would suggest – that all children exhibit a set of relative strengths and weaknesses that correspond with the notion of multiple intelligences. The areas examined were – numbers, science, music, language, visual arts, movement, and social.

This early research was complex, but it yielded several seemingly incontestable conclusions. First, understanding the domain strengths and weaknesses of a student is necessary in order to most effectively approach any learning task. In current pedagogical language, this is the neurobiological imperative behind what is called differentiated instruction. And second, the domain strengths of a student can be very effective allies in learning something in another realm entirely. For example, Gardner cites a student whose exceptional strength in visual arts was a great asset in succeeding in a game that primarily focused on logical inference skills.

It is remarkable to consider the extent to which the pioneers of progressive education intuitively understood the things Gardner formalized 150 years later.

Johann Heinrich Pestalozzi was among the first educators to think of the "whole child." While he did not directly address spheres of intelligence, in hindsight he was attentive to inter-personal and intrapersonal intelligence, bodily-kinesthetic intelligence, naturalistic, and existential intelligence. Among Pestalozzi's great virtues was his focus on teaching the poor, and the very progressive notion of education as a right for all. The German Friedrich Froebel, who coined the word "kinder-garten" and gave to posterity his idea of "Froebel Gifts," was keenly aware of attending to the multiple intelligences Gardner later proposed. His kindergarten included singing, dancing, gardening and self-directed play in each school day.

Chapter Seven

Education and the Arts

In light of the neurobiological evidence for attending to multiple ways of being intelligent, and the inarguable benefits of rich sensory experience, there are few things more baffling than the short shrift given the arts in schools. While this is a general trend, it is particularly true in poor communities, often communities of color, where budget cuts and a government-mandated testing regimen leave little time for what too many people regard as frills.

For the purpose of this discussion, I define the arts as visual and performing arts – the latter to include music and theater. Many organizations are dedicated to advancing the role of arts in education, but are swimming against a tide of public policy that relegates arts to the periphery – or all the way out the door. One sad example is found in a 2014 report [64] from the New York City Comptroller, who found that spending on arts supplies and equipment fell by 84 percent from 2006 to 2013, 20 percent of the city's public schools had no arts teachers, and that these artless schools were concentrated in poor neighborhoods.

One organization trying to reverse this trend was founded in 1989, initially called Center for Arts in the Basic Curriculum. The group has made a compelling philosophical, biological, psychological and pragmatic case for the importance of the arts in the education of all children.

This group, now known as Arts/Learning, was associated with Howard Gardner since its inception. They offer a wealth of research that supports the cognitive benefits of arts programs in schools.

I applaud the work they've done and continue to do, but I am concerned when any argument is based solely or primarily on pragmatic benefits. For example, I cringe when proponents of sane environmental policy focus only on "it's good for business" arguments. It may be true that sound environmental practices will be good for a business's bottom line. But if we appeal to corporations to behave ethically only because it will benefit them, then we concede that they are free to behave unethically if the promise of self-interest is not true. We must protect the Earth even if it's economically disadvantageous to do so.

And this caution applies equally to the arts. Music, dance, theater, film and the fine arts are indeed wise elements of a school curriculum, for the reasons Gardner and Arts/Learning explicate. But we should not have to justify the arts solely because they produce better outcomes – however outcomes are defined. The arts should be at the center of a school because the arts are essential to the human experience. If the outcomes a school intends do not include nourishment for the spirit and soul, then the school should reconsider its purposes. Outcomes-based pragmatism is choking life out of schools and society. But it is, once again, a false choice. The arts not only gladden the heart and enliven the soul. They tickle the synapses in our brains and provide another powerful way to understand language, grasp mathematical concepts, visualize a scientific principle, and stir our knowledge and information into deep understanding.

Music

Recent discoveries about the power of music may be the best news since the revelations that red wine and chocolate are good for one's health. Such felicitous discoveries might make the most insistent atheist consider the possibility of a beneficent power at work in the universe. As with wine and chocolate, music's power goes far beyond pleasure. Abundant evidence shows that music is among the most powerful ingredients in other learning including, but not limited to, language development and mathematics.

Research suggests that music predated language as a means of human communication. The tonal nature of speech and the musical dialogue among other species hint at music's essential power.

Essential power. I will never forget Christmas Eve in 1970, when I was working as a mental health assistant in a psychiatric hospital. Mr. Henderson, a patient at that time, suffered from what was termed "chronic brain syndrome," meaning that no one knew what was wrong with him. He had no language, and on his best days he could eat with a spoon. He never spoke or made eye contact. He was subject to fits of wild frustration with no observable cause, so we managed him with great caution. He was a large man. When he seemed calm, we would try to normalize his evenings, sitting him among others during social activities. He never engaged or seemed to notice people or things. On this night, he was quite calm and I decided to take a risk and bring him to the lobby, as local children were coming by to sing carols to the patients. I was his regular companion on such occasions, being among the few capable of restraining him if needed. The lobby was decorated with sparse white lights and a crooked little Christmas tree. Light snow was falling as the children entered the lobby, red-cheeked and a bit nervous – it was a psychiatric hospital after all. They began singing. "Jingle Bells, Jingle Bells, Jingle all the way ..." Then, "Silent Night, Holy Night ..." I glanced at Mr. Henderson. His eyes were wide, brimming with tears. Amid the stubble and spittle of his life-less face his lips began to move. Silently, certainly, he mouthed, "Holy infant, tender and mild, sleep in heavenly peace, sleep in heavenly peace." I squeezed his hand, but he never spoke again.

Before continuing with the neurobiological rationale for a lively music program, a few words for the impractical. The late Reverend William Sloane Coffin was my good friend and recital partner (he, piano, I, violin) for a dozen years. During one rehearsal he remarked that performing Mozart made him much more nervous than any sermon he ever preached. After a brief, reflective pause he mused that perhaps that was because music is a much more direct expression of the divine than anything he might ever think to say. Although Bill and I shared an appreciation of many things – beautiful phrases, red wine, and chocolate, among others – I didn't share his belief in the divine, at least not in a literal sense. But I seldom have a more powerful connection to the ineffable than in the good company of music.

Chopin Nocturnes absorbed at age five beneath my mother's piano carry more emotional power than any other memories of those early years. The opening chords of a Bach Prelude played at my father's memorial service will forever evoke unbidden tears. This is no elitist phenomenon, for the saccharine theme from the saccharine movie "Love Story" calls up lovely images and feelings from early in my marriage that may be otherwise inaccessible. Even a song as inane as the 1960s hit *96 Tears* by ? and the Mysterians carries a flood of teenage emotions along with its dreadful two-chord keyboard drone.

Music should thus be a significant part of every school day, if for no other reason than it gives great pleasure, but music also provides a medium in which life experiences are stored for future enjoyment, perhaps with more power than any other mechanism.

The most widely discussed role of music in learning arose from a phenomenon called the "Mozart Effect." [65] This phrase, trademarked by the author Don Campbell, represents a now largely discredited claim that music – Mozart in particular, piano concerti in the particularly particular – increases IQ, adds points to SAT scores, stimulates learning, and fosters creativity and imagination. On further examination, this "effect" lasts about fifteen minutes and is related to very fleeting mood changes or temporary arousal. Nonetheless, millions bought Campbell's books and put Mozart concerti on the home stereo hour after hour. There are worse things of course. In fact, as one who loves Mozart piano concerti, almost everything else is worse.

Many benefits of music have been apparent for decades, if

not centuries. Learning to play an instrument requires discipline, good time management, development of fine motor skills, persistence, patience, focus, and many other traits that have value far beyond the musical skill itself. The sequencing and scaffolding activities demanded by learning an instrument are applicable to nearly all kinds of learning. Music students also learn a great deal from ensemble experiences, ranging from simple duets to full orchestras. Learning to match intonation, shape phrases, defer when appropriate, hear the whole along with the parts – these are all complex and powerfully important cognitive and social skills. These skills are even more complex in jazz, where improvisation demands an amazingly complex set of cognitive and motor skills. Making music with others is a very high order process.

Even more fascinating are the indications that music may be intimately, arguably inextricably, tied to the neural process of acquiring language. Daniel J. Levitin's fine book, *This Is Your Brain on Music: The Science of a Human Obsession*, [66] is a good and accessible introduction to the fascinating world of the neurobiology of music. Among other things, Levitin observes the neural basis of emotions aroused by music, connecting the roles of the cerebellum, amygdala and frontal lobe of the brain. The collaboration among these primitive and highly developed brain functions suggests the complex place of music in memory, cognition, emotion, and even that critical student skill, executive function.

Other intriguing suggestions of the essential role of music come from the Duke University Center for Cognitive Neuroscience. [67] Among other things they discovered is that the 12-tone intervals found in much of the world's music are identical to the tonality in most human speech, across such linguistic ranges as English to Mandarin. This hints that music is embedded at some deep, perhaps pre-language stratum of the human brain.

Even more current and directly germane is a Northwestern University study published several years ago in *Nature Reviews Neuroscience*. [68] This work provides substantial evidence that playing a musical instrument "significantly enhances the brainstem's sensitivity to sound encoding skills." Nina Kraus, the study's senior author writes, "Our findings underscore the pervasive impact of musical training on neurological development."

In the *Annals of the New York Academy of Sciences*, [69] Diego Minciacchi of the University of Florence provides an even broader endorsement. "Musical performance is the realm in which humans produce the most elaborate integration processes, involving perceptual, cognitive, emotional, and motor skills."

Harvard neurologist Gottfried Schlaug adds:

... music training might enhance spatial reasoning because music notation itself is spatial. Mathematical skills may well be enhanced by music learning because understanding rhythmic notation actually requires math specific skills such as pattern recognition and an understanding of proportion, ratio, fractions, and subdivision...

Phonemic awareness skills may be improved by music training because both music and language processing require the ability to segment streams of sound into small perceptual units. [70]

Deep at the foundations of authentic human experience is

music, that magical precursor of language, mathematics and love. From the limits of recorded human history to the breath-taking songs of warblers and whales, music may be the most universal and compelling form of expression – across time, species and experience. The thought that music can be and is abandoned in schools is heartbreaking. It's also just dumb.

Far too many well-intentioned parents of young children are engaged in a daily battle of wills, exhorting their children to do more homework and memorize more things for tests. Relax! Pour a glass of red wine (for yourself), break out the dark chocolate (for you and the kids), sing with your children or listen to some good music. If the neighbors wonder what's going on, tell them you're preparing your kids for college. And you might live long enough to sing with your great-grandchildren, too.

Visual Arts

Much of the argument for music in education is true in similar ways for the visual arts. An article in the Harvard Education Review discussed the work of Eric Jensen, author of *Arts with the Brain in Mind*:

> *Regarding the visual arts, Jensen concludes, 'Research from the studies discussed in this book and the experience of countless classroom educators support the view that visual arts have strong positive cognitive, emotional, social, collaborative, and neurological effects.'* [71]

Jensen and others report many positive benefits associated with visual arts. Many of these qualities are common with other performing arts as well. Students demonstrate stronger academic skills and better critical capacities. Jensen also writes extensively about what he calls the kinesthetic arts, specifically dance:

Here's the bottom line on the kinesthetic arts: The research, the theory, and real-world classroom experience clearly support sustaining or increasing the role of movement in learning. [71]

Dee Dickinson, who founded New Horizons for Learning, which is now associated with Johns Hopkins University, is another astute proponent of the arts in education, particularly the idea that the arts are tools that facilitate learning for students who are strong in visual and kinesthetic realms. Dickinson cites work done by Lynn O'Brien, whose research shows that students who learn best through listening are only about 15% of the population. Students who are strongest in the visual realm are about 40% of the population. This should not be surprising, given the extent and range of visual sensation in our environment. From an evolutionary point of view, it seems intuitive that humans learn a great deal from visual stimuli. O'Brien also reports that students who learn best in the kinesthetic sense comprise about 45% of the population. As Dickinson writes, "*Abstractions presented in words and numbers may not be easily understood without manipulatives or concrete examples.*" [72]

The visual arts therefore develop critically important tools for students who are strong visual or kinesthetic learners – and these are the majority of students. Addressing these strengths is not only important to the arts, but can enhance learning in all parts of the curriculum.

Mona Brookes, founder of Monart Drawing Schools and author of *Drawing with Children,* uses the visual arts to increase letter recognition and reading readiness. She reports that:

... teachers also noticed that the motivation to read expanded when the children   drew characters and subjects from their books. Drawing the content of science,   geography, and social studies lessons resulted in noticeable differences in speed of learning and retention. When teachers used the abstract design lessons to teach math concepts, they witnessed children break through conceptual blocks with ease while having fun. [73]

Theater

Theater is equally important, for reasons similar to those cited for music and the visual arts – it is visual, kinesthetic, active and engaging. But theater has an additional power – the development of empathy and understanding. I illustrate with just one example from Calhoun's own program. I wrote about it for Huffington Post a few years ago:

The ten or so "seniors" entering the Calhoun School's theater on Monday afternoon were greeted with a round of cheers by the fourth grade; it wasn't their first encounter. These were not high school seniors, but a group of Upper Westside Manhattan residents from a Senior Center down the street who came to watch a set of brief performances.

Our fourth graders and their older friends became acquainted through Calhoun's community service program. As with any good community engagement, our relationship with this Center is not an act of charity or noblesse oblige on the part of a wealthy private school and its privileged students. To the contrary, through these kinds of relationships we receive far more than we give.

Fourth grade teachers extended this relationship into a piece of exemplary curriculum. Our elder neighbors were invited to write stories of their own childhood – focusing on when they themselves were approximately 10, the age of our students. Our teachers and students then carefully crafted the stories into short plays. The students played all the parts, including the stories' narrators, the once 10-year-olds who are now the octogenarian and nonagenarian friends seated in the front row.

It was a delightful hour. The students' performances ranged from blushing innocence to soaring eloquence (and frequent irreverence). There were no sets, no fancy costumes and the students needed occasional prompts from a teacher in the wings. It was mighty endearing; the fourth graders make my heart melt. Of course, second graders and 11th graders make my heart melt too, so maybe I'm not the most dispassionate critic.

The stories were highly varied, capturing the innocence of a first kiss, evoking the day that Hitler invaded Poland, or expressing the universal thrill of childhood anticipation, as a girl anxiously awaited a longed-for gift of a doll.

A particularly poignant piece illustrated the reality of life for immigrant families in New York City in the early 20th century. A girl and her younger sister went forth too boldly into their new neighborhood where they knew neither the language nor the streets. They were guided safely home by the kind attention of a nameless neighbor in their strange new country.

I needn't elaborate on the elder friends' reactions to the performance – you might imagine. There were laughs and tears; they were on the edge of their seats. And after the performance, the actors and the audience enjoyed platters of cookies with milk. Their mutual affection was very, very real.

It is easy to like this and equally easy to underestimate its power. The student performances required empathy, as does all good theater. These fourth graders became immigrant children lost in an overwhelming city. They inhabited another world and another time. They learned what was different then, but, far more importantly, they learned what was the same. They learned that the gray, wrinkly friends in the front row were once kids, just like them, with the same fears, hopes, and silly senses of humor. They realized that the distance between 10 and 90 is only an arm's length, if you open your heart and mind.

In the test-obsessed environment driven by current public policy, along with persistent attacks on teachers, what teacher could risk taking time to do something like this?

Teachers with 30 kids in the classroom can't do it. Teachers who are told to use more technology so that they can "deliver content" with more furious efficiency can't do it. Teachers who are handed a dull script about the day's state standard can't do it. The teachers whose jobs and lives are dependent on raising test scores can't do it. The teachers of earnest little fourth graders in charter schools, lined up in their blazers and skirts, certainly can't or won't do it.

Those teachers don't have time for giggles. They can't pause long enough for their students to share a glass of milk and a cookie with 85-year-olds who they never imagined to have had a first kiss or gotten lost and confused, just as they have been. There isn't time to learn that World War II was not just an event in a textbook, but was a real experience that deeply affected the lives of children who loved beautiful dolls or dreamt of building perfect igloos.

This one experience provided more real learning than months of preparation for a test, whose questions and answers are sure to be forgotten by the next week. The fourth grade students in this project and their neighborhood friends will never forget it. Nor will I.

A similar invocation of empathy and learning through theater emerged in a Calhoun Upper School theater production several years ago. Students staged a powerful production of *The Laramie Project,* a play revisiting the Wyoming murder of gay college student Matthew Shepard. The performances were stunning – not only because of their high level of craft, but also because of the capacity for empathy that allowed the students to inhabit the characters they played. And not all of the characters in The Laramie Project are sympathetic. The play includes Matthew's murderers, the town's unrepentant homophobes, and longtime Wyoming folks who sought to reconcile the horror of this murder with their previously unchallenged sense of themselves. It was remarkable to watch teenagers capture the complexity and humanity of these folks, who could have been simple caricatures in a lesser production.

Chapter Eight

Broken Windows and Broken Windows

Relationships and the Nature of a School Community

As with the other principles of progressive education, the power of relationships in learning is affirmed by theory, observation and, especially in recent decades, a substantial and growing body of research. The effect of human relationships in schools is equally important between and among children and between and among children and adults.

It is not surprising that progressive schools springing from a humanist impulse actually value human relationships. Although I don't suggest that conventional schools are inhumane, the nature of student-teacher relationships is different in intent and practice. It is this difference, along with the economies of scale championed by neoconservative reformers, which accounts for the attitude that class size doesn't matter. This is among the most important distinctions between progressive and conventional schools.

In the early 20th century and again in the 1960's and 1990's, a more industrial approach to education prevailed for political, not educational reasons. Like Ford Motor Company assembly lines, this mechanistic way of looking at schools has its own notion of automation – standardize the curriculum, standardize the lesson plans and materials, standardize the assessments, and the system will operate quite well with minimal staffing.

If this way of education had merit, the reformers would be right. Instruction delivered directly from a syllabus, poured directly into little heads, will work equally well with a classroom of 15 or 30 or, in higher education, even 450. Why waste money on expensive teachers and their fringe benefits? Technology proponents, who love the scalability offered by online programs, enthusiastically embrace this modern iteration of the factory model. Not only is lean staffing possible, now there is no real need for classrooms either.

When teacher and student relationships are sacrificed in the service of a cheaper factory model, the results are training, not education.

Once again, the early progressive theorists were prescient. From Pestalozzi and Froebel through Dewey and Parker, relationships within the school community were of central importance. All of them espoused a democratic environment in which adults have comfortable, peer-like relationships with students, rather than formal authoritarian roles. All subsequent research has reaffirmed the importance of both the relationships and the nature of the relationships. More recently, both Lev Vygotsky and Jerome Bruner advanced the idea of social-development and adult-child social interaction as the primary medium for language development.

The power of relationships has also been affirmed by the rapidly advancing knowledge of child development and brain biology. A researcher with a Calhoun connection, Clancy Blair, is a psychologist who specializes in school readiness and emotional regulation. Two of Blair's children are Calhoun graduates. In a paper titled, "School Readiness: Integrating Cognition and Emotion in a Neurobiological Conceptualization of Children's Functioning at School Entry", [74] Blair makes a more complex argument than I can summarize here, but among his conclusions is that school readiness is highly correlated with warm, supportive relationships with adults, both in and out of early childhood education settings.

Sondra Birch and Gary Ladd at the University of Illinois make an equally compelling case in their *Journal of School Psychology* article titled, "The Teacher-Child Relationship and Children's Early School Adjustment." [75] Their research was extensive and looked at many dimensions of school performance and its correlation with positive, intimate relationships with teachers. The details are unnecessary for the purpose of this book, but they conclude their study with this:

... the quality of children's teacher-child relationships may have far-reaching significance in terms of the various educational trajectories that children follow throughout their schooling experience.

The research pointing to the importance of relationships in early childhood is reinforced by evidence aplenty that this dynamic continues through subsequent stages of child development and school. Early 20th Century theorists like psychologist Erik Erikson and psychiatrist Margaret Mahler noted the critical importance of separation-individuation. They studied and described the stages through which infants, babies and toddlers progress when developing a sense of self and their place in the world. Contemporary psychologists suggest that an analogous sequence of steps toward individuation occur during adolescence. At this time, the relationships formed with non-familial adults are crucial.

Jacquelynne Eccles, a psychologist at the University of Michigan to whom I referred when discussing intrinsic motivation, writes:

> *For example, the structure of junior high schools reduces opportunities for adolescents to form close relationships with their teachers at precisely the point in the early adolescents' development when they have a great need for guidance and support from non-familial adults. Because most junior high schools are larger than elementary schools, and instruction is organized by department, teachers work with several groups of students a day and seldom teach a student for more than one year. Interactions between teacher and student usually focus on the academic content of what is being taught or on disciplinary issues. Teachers at this level tend to feel less effective as teachers. These structures can undermine the sense of community and trust between early adolescents and their teachers – leading in turn to a greater reliance by teachers on authoritarian control and increased alienation among*

the students. [76]

I should emphasize that the nature of the relationships is critically important. One characteristic of many, perhaps most, progressive schools is that teachers and students are on a first name basis. This convention may seem unimportant, but it has very deep implications for learning. It is also a source of pleasure and occasional amusement.

When first coming to Calhoun I was curious about this practice. In all the schools I attended, as well as my children's schools, teachers were Mr., Mrs., Ms., Sir, Ma'am, Dr. or some other form of formal address. "Hi Steve!" felt odd – for a few days. Soon enough it was the other that felt odd. Now I instinctively cringe if anyone calls me "Mister," wondering what I've done wrong.

Adaptation is not so easy for everyone. Some years ago a girl came to Calhoun in middle school. She and her family had moved from North Carolina to New York City. I met with her and her parents in the admission process. Using her well-honed Southern refinement, she addressed me as "Dr. Nelson." I encouraged her to call me Steve, telling her it was the Calhoun practice to use first names. I didn't disabuse her of the "Dr." part, although I have no doctorate. I figured I'd just leave that alone, since she would quickly come to "Steve."

Whenever I would encounter this lovely young woman, I would say, "Hi Amy!" and she would cheerfully respond, "Hi Dr. Nelson!" I'd invite her to call me Steve. Next time, "Hi Dr. Nelson!" Finally, after several months of gentle encouragement, Amy took a big leap. "Hi Amy!" "Hi Dr. Steve!" It was the best she could do, and Dr. Steve I remained until Amy left for boarding school a few years later.

By contrast, Isabelle, Taylor, Julia and Peri starting calling me "Stevie" when they were in the second grade. I haven't the faintest idea why. I pointed out to them that no one had ever called me Stevie, including my mother. They were not persuaded. They called me Stevie through and beyond graduation several years ago. And I called them Isabelle-ie, Julia-ie, Taylor-ie and Peri-ie. I enjoyed encountering one or more of them when touring visitors, who looked at me with confusion after hearing these students cheerfully call out, "Hi Stevie." I figured if it were really off-putting to the visitors, they would find another school more to their liking.

Those who are unfamiliar with this kind of school setting will often express skepticism. How, they wonder, can any kind of order be maintained with this lack of authority? Don't kids need to respect their teachers, and especially the head of school? When questioned about this facet of our school, I ask a question in return. "Have you ever respected any person more because they insisted on being addressed with a formal title?" I am always wary of anyone who is too concerned about what he or she is called. I tend to respect people a bit less if they are insistent on a title. In fact it's an almost perfect inverse correlation – the more someone cares about it, the less admiration I have.

Children are not stupid. They too can spot the insecurity of a title-conscious person a mile away. They will follow the convention, but it is a mistake to believe that real respect is based on formality. The lack of formality in a progressive school actually strengthens and clarifies the notion of respect. Respect is something to be earned through wisdom, kindness, consistency, fairness, humor, and other qualities. The respect garnered through formality or rules is shallow. Once out of the view of the authority figure, children will reveal the way they really feel. This sets up a cynical mistrust and a barrier between student and teacher that can inhibit the interactions that positively affect the learning experience – for both the student and the teacher.

The warmth and familiarity that develop between kids and adults in a progressive school doesn't confuse the kids. I know from sad experience that I can be Steve (or Stevie) one moment, and the Head of School who must make a disciplinary decision the next. When I've had to deal with very difficult situations with students I love, the closeness is an asset, not a liability. They trust and understand the very different role I must assume. It is impossible for them to dismiss my consternation as distant, unfair or rigid, because they know I care deeply about them.

Relationships between and among students are equally important. The word "community" is both misused and over-used. Nearly any assembly of humans gets the name these days. But in progressive theory and practice the meaning of community is quite specific and intentional. Community in this context implies interdependence, not competition. It is among the reasons that progressive schools frequently eschew grades, class ranks or academic honors. The spirit is cooperative. When children grow in this kind of school community, there tends to be a greater appreciation for others' accomplishments and abilities. Progressive schools also focus on matters of equity, inclusion rather than exclusion, and the importance of empathy.

Much has been written about the power of communities or groups working cooperatively. Scott Page, in his 2007 book, *The Difference: How the Power of Diversity Creates Better Groups, Firms, Schools, and Societies*, [77] makes a strong case for the superiority of interactive group work – that collective wisdom is, as he writes, more than the sum of the individual parts.

Martin Nystrand, Professor of English at the University of Wisconsin-Madison, was the first researcher to look specifically at the dynamic classroom discussion. His 2001 paper, "Questions in Time: Investigating the Structure and Dynamics of Unfolding Classroom Discourse", [78] is an important affirmation of the power of discussion, and further strengthens the progressive notions of learning through collaboration and active engagement. In his words:

> ... *gifted teachers enliven the learning experience by engaging their students in active inquiry, in contrast to the more typical teaching environment, which is characterized by rote memorization and recitation of instructional materials.*

Nystrand's work revealed how rare this dynamic is. In a study of 2,400 students in 60 schools, he found that a typical teacher "allows" only about 3 minutes/hour of discussion among students. Even among those 3 minutes, much of the "discussion" is teacher-directed, eliciting what the teacher is seeking. And, not surprisingly, the poorer the students in the school, the fewer opportunities they have for discussion. This is a part of the collateral damage of buying into the "class size doesn't matter" mythology. Class size matters a great deal if the aim is real education. At Calhoun, and in progressive schools everywhere, the very best classes, rarely larger than 15, are led by students, with the teacher afforded 3 minutes to frame and guide the discussion!

I've referred several times to advances in cognitive science that confirm the instincts and observations of progressive educators over several centuries. I mentioned both dopamine and cortisol in Chapter 4 in describing Jerome Bruner's warnings about "too much too soon" in early childhood education. Both dopamine and cortisol merit more thorough examination of their role in explaining why a progressive environment is a better educational environment.

While stimulating school activities may slightly increase cortisol levels and thereby facilitate memory development, the negative effects of high levels of cortisol are well known, and neuroscientists have known for some time that chronic stress, lasting for weeks or months, impairs the cell communication that is critical to learning and memory. Researchers at the University of California, Irvine discovered that this effect is equally pronounced with short-term stress. This is because the hormones released under stress rapidly disintegrate the dendrites (connections between neurons) that facilitate the synapses that process and store information and memories. Another study, conducted by the National Institute on Aging, found that cortisol disrupts the hippocampus, the region of the brain most responsible for learning and short-term memory. In her summary of "Dopamine and Stress Responses" Robin Wood-Moen notes that, "Those who are exposed to chronically stressful environments tend to exhibit memory deficits, poor concentration and have inadequate blood flow to the brain." [79] Scores of similar sources verify the negative effects excessive stress has on learning.

While the following examples are analogous (not identical) to school environments, there is broader evidence of the cognitive effects of stress. Charles Murray and Richard J. Herrnstein's 1994 book, *Bell Curve, Intelligence and Class Structure in American Life*, [80] raised the offensive notion of racial inferiority. Their research ignored the deleterious effects of stress and low self esteem on IQ. Many scholars have debunked any notion of actual intelligence differences among and between races or ethnic groups. A1998 article in *The New York Times* provided an excellent summary of IQ and race or caste. [81]

In *The New York Times* on December 2014, columnist David Brooks provided another example:

> *Sugar cane farmers in India receive most of their income once a year, at harvest time. In the weeks before harvest, when they are poor and stressed, they score 10 points lower on I.Q. tests than in the weeks after. If you schedule fertilizer purchase decisions and their children's school enrollment decisions during the weeks after harvest, they will make more farsighted choices than at other times of the year. This simple policy change is based on an under-standing of how poverty depletes mental resources.* [82]

High stakes tests, long hours of unnecessary homework, sleep deprivation, and constant competition and pressure as part of the daily diet in many, many schools create high stress, which is unquestionably damaging. So why on Earth do we celebrate schools engaging in these practices?

On the other side of the dopamine/cortisol relationship, the function of dopamine as a critical neurotransmitter is clearly understood. The presence of dopamine in the brain is important in the process of storing memories, affecting how the hippo-campus builds accurate memories of past events. The implica-tions and importance of "building accurate memories of past events" should be self-evident in terms of learning and schools.

Columbia University's Daphna Shohamy and colleagues have done important research on this topic. They report that:

... dopamine ensures that memories are relevant and accessible for future adaptive behavior, a concept we refer to as 'adaptive memory'. Understanding adaptive memory at biological and psychological levels helps to resolve a fundamental challenge in memory research: explaining what is remembered, and why. [83]

This creates an interesting self-reinforcing phenomenon. The more motivated or interested we are in an activity, the more dopamine is produced. More dopamine assists in building memory. And particularly in terms of this chapter's emphasis on the importance of relationships, dopamine is produced when one is in the presence of friends or loved ones – in all positive human relationships including, perhaps especially, in school.

So natural, warm relationships are critically important in schools, but not just because they make school more pleasant and fun. These relationships also enable the production of dopamine, which is essential to learning and memory formation. So now what was it you thought was good about a stern, punitive, competitive school environment? In lay terms, this is a win-win, and is all the science anyone needs to know in order to intentionally avoid tedium, fear or intimidation in the classroom.

Relationships with students should also be among, perhaps primarily among, the reasons anyone would want to work in a school. Yet I am equal parts amazed and disappointed to discover how many teachers and, especially, administrators, appear to have no real affection for children – or even dislike them. Kids are eager for relationships with adults. Kids like Carol.

In the fall of 1998, during my first weeks as Head of Calhoun, I visited a kindergarten class. The teacher, a wonderful woman named Lil Lulkin, invited me to sit in a circle on the floor among the children, just to get acquainted. The kids were curious about the strange adult but, as is invariably true in a warm, progressive environment, they were not intimidated. Lil said, "Steve is the new head of school. Do you know what that is?" "He's like the principal?" "He is the boss of you?" "He owns the school!" We gradually decided that my job was to keep everybody safe and happy, a job description I'll gladly accept.

One girl, Carol, said absolutely nothing. She sat just a bit back, on the edge of the circle, and stared at me. It wasn't a blank stare. I could tell she was sizing me up. I could see little shifts in her affect as I bantered and joked with the other kids, but she didn't offer anything at all to the conversation. This went on for about 10 minutes. Then, suddenly, Carol stood up and walked toward me. Without uttering a word, she leaned down and pressed her face against mine. Nose to nose, forehead to forehead, eyes to eyes. She held that position for a few seconds, then pulled her head back and threw her arms around me and squeezed me in a lovely hug.

She walked back to her place in the circle and joined in the conversation. I haven't enjoyed scrutiny that much since the time in 1970 when I came to believe I was on the FBI watch list because of subscribing to a progressive magazine.

Calhoun's early childhood program is in a building called Little Calhoun, some 8 or 9 blocks from Big Calhoun, where my office was at the time. Carol's older sibling was a student in 2nd or 3rd grade, and Carol would accompany her mother to pick up the older sibling, as the older kids' dismissal was a bit later. Every day Carol would come to my office as her mother went to the second floor for pick-up. She would walk in, give me a hug, and walk out. No words exchanged. It was just our daily routine. I am acutely attuned to children who might display intimacy or affection in a way that shouldn't be encouraged. Any thoughtful teacher knows when clinging or excessive physical contact is ill advised, but Carol's daily visit had no such overtones. She just figured (correctly) that we were friends and a goodbye hug was a nice way to end the day.

Sometimes Carol would come and find my office empty. Other times she would bounce down the stairs to my office, peer through the glass-paned French doors, and see that I had company, perhaps a small meeting. She always waited for a signal. If I smiled and gestured her in, she would slide the door open, give the hug, turn around and leave, in our customary wordless fashion. If I gently shook my head "no," she would put her arms up, give me an "air hug," and bounce back up the stairs.

The next year, or the year after, Carol's family returned to Europe and I haven't seen her since. Who wouldn't want a job where things like that happen?

But my enjoyment is not the point of emphasizing relationships. There is no school dynamic as important as the relationships between and among students and their teachers. Perhaps the progressive distinction in this regard is that the relationships are not based primarily on age or authority. The emotional distance established through conventional hierarchy and large class size inhibits learning.

Our cultural archetype of teacher is "master," or "sage on a stage." Usually the teacher is seen as a serious, sometimes stern, adult who must maintain control over children and the classroom. "I'm not your friend," declares the master, peering over reading spectacles. I suppose if we believe a rigorous education is desirable, and we hold to the "no pain no gain" belief about schools and learning, then it's no surprise that teachers are supposed to be some version of Vince Lombardi or Margaret Thatcher.

The progressive concept of a teacher has always been more of a peer relationship – a guide, a mentor and, yes, a friend. There are many cultural forms this can take, but the power of genuine, non-threatening relationships is central. The contrast between a progressive way of viewing children and a conventional viewpoint is quite striking. Examining two very different schools, admittedly toward the opposite ends of a continuum, may be instructive.

There are many examples of how children are valued and treated in progressive schools. Among the more radical is Summerhill, founded in England in 1921 by A.S. Neill. During the late 19th and early 20th centuries, progressive schools gained some foothold in both Europe and the United States. Among the surviving schools, the King Alfred School in Hampstead (London), England is one with which I am most familiar, having spoken at a 2009 conference at the school. I also spent an enjoyable day on the campus, learning about the school and its fascinating history. King Alfred is still a progressive school in most ways, including the role of students in governing and in the relative freedom they enjoy. I mention King Alfred because A.S. Neill taught there from his military discharge in 1917 until his founding of Summerhill in 1921.

Summerhill is among the early examples of a truly democratic school. Neill rejected the idea of adult authority, believing that children have full rights, are not "owned" by parents or teachers, and should not be forced to do anything against their own will, except as a matter of consideration for others. To say that his view was controversial in the 1920's would be a dramatic understatement. It remains a rather radical notion to most parents and educators.

Summerhill does not require students to attend classes unless they so choose. Among the important results of this nearly century-long experiment is that the children do indeed attend classes. As all progressive educators know, children are innately curious until and unless we beat it out of them by making school tedious and stressful. In his own book, *Summerhill, A Radical Approach to Child Rearing*, [3] Neill reports that the record for not attending class was, at the time of his writing in 1960, three years, held by a girl who had come to Summerhill from a convent. In Neill's view, three years was about the right amount of time for recovery from time in a convent. It bears noting that Neill was an atheist, which may have colored his view of convents!

Students at Summerhill are also responsible for making and monitoring the rules. Neill reports one particularly humorous incident in which a six year-old boy had come to him to confess that he'd broken a window. Just before then the students had chosen to boycott the School Government and refused to stand for election. Neill, I assume with tongue planted in cheek, therefore declared himself Dictator.

This made the students quite unhappy, resulting in some group harassment of the cook, who promptly closed the kitchen and quit. When Neill suggested to the boy that he would have to pay for the window, as it was Neill's private property and destroying another's property was against the rules the government adopted, the boy did him one better. He told Neill that dictatorships are not government, and without government there is no notion of private property and therefore he had no obligation to pay. The boy returned a short time later to report that he had broken 17 windows. Eventually a kind man who heard and enjoyed the story paid for the windows and the School Government (and lunch!) was restored.

I cite Summerhill not because I believe it to be the optimal school environment, but to reinforce a counter-intuitive point. Many students from Summerhill experienced great academic success in university and most reported a very high level of accomplishment, life satisfaction, and independence. While Summerhill and other free or democratic schools are at the far end of a progressive continuum, their students are successful in the ways that matter most, as confirmed by the Eight Year Study to which I referred earlier in Chapter 2.

The contrasting example is the KIPP charter school chain, also previously cited in Chapter 2. Two young Ivy League graduates, Mike Feinberg and Dave Levin, founded KIPP schools. Their schools have been both widely praised and deeply scorned, depending on your point of view. They are held up as examples of the power of school choice and the benefits of liberation from public school policy and teacher unions. They have been partially credited with the supposed "miracle in New Orleans," where, after Hurricane Katrina, public schools were almost entirely taken over by the charter/choice move- ment. Many astute investigators have revealed that the alleged "miracle" is tainted by shifting standards of accountability, expelling high percentages of students and other education reform sleights of hand.

KIPP schools, like most urban charters, have a very strict

disciplinary philosophy. Sadly, KIPP has been enthusiastically endorsed by Paul Tough, the bestselling author of *How Children Succeed; Grit, Curiosity, and the Hidden Power of Character* [84] and its sequel, *Helping Children Succeed: What Works and Why*. [85]

Tough, whose thesis is interesting, albeit overstated, (and whose name is ironically apt) has fathered an epidemic of "grit" seeking. He contends that perseverance and other similar so-called character traits are as important to school success as intelligence. This point of view has some merit, but the policies and actions it has inspired in KIPP and similar schools are discouraging.

So What About Grit?

While this chapter is primarily about the importance and nature of relationships, it is relevant to comment on the grit phenomenon a bit more extensively, since it is so very fashionable these days.

Tough's books are the most popular manifestation of the grit fad, but grit has many advocates in psychological and pedagogical circles. Angela Duckworth, a psychologist at the University of Pennsylvania, is well known for her "gritty" TED talk, [86] and for her presentations at conferences and schools around the country. Stanford psychologist Carol Dweck is another notable advocate for the grit cause, although her work is more broadly directed toward motivational mindsets.

Even Howard Gardner has joined the grit parade. In a short presentation at the Harvard Graduate School of Education, [87] Gardner cites grit in a talk arguing that "wits" (multiple intelligences) and "grit" can and should be turned toward Good Work for the benefit of humanity. That's a hard ambition to refute.

In the sense that Duckworth, Dweck and Gardner propose, the notion of grit is helpful in that it differentiates between the separate roles that intelligence and determination have in learning. Dweck's research shows, for example, that children who are praised for intelligence may become risk averse, thereby inhibiting learning. Children praised for effort are much less likely to avoid challenge – in fact her research shows that they are more likely to seek it out.

Simply stated, the grit theory decouples an individual's potential from only their intelligence. This is certainly a hopeful and helpful way of thinking about children and schools. But Duckworth, in particular, seems to embrace an IQ view of intelligence, thus looking at IQ and grit as operating in a closed system. Without accounting for multiple intelligences and their complex intersection with perseverance, her analysis is incomplete.

While it is valuable to recognize that perseverance, motivation and determination are distinct from intelligence(s) and are important to both school and life success, the grit bandwagon has a dangerous collateral effect. It takes one flawed idea – "you aren't smart enough to do well in school," and compounds it with another flawed idea – "you aren't gritty enough to do well in school."

These notions, in combination, relieve policy makers and educators of the responsibility to look at their practices and expectations. The first responsibility of good educators, particularly in the early years, is to make learning so dynamic, interesting and fun that it would take grit to turn away! Focusing on the importance of grit allows a teacher or policy maker to design any manner of unimaginative, rote, tedious or punitive exercise and then blame a student's indifference, inattention or failure on their lack of grit.

KIPP schools are a case in point.

Students in KIPP schools wear uniforms, walk silently in single file lines from class to class, and are disciplined for even the smallest infraction. It is a school-based version of the "broken windows" policing philosophy, which claims that the best way to control crime is to aggressively criminalize every small act. Arrest the window breaker, the theory goes, and murders will go down. As this has played out in places like NYC, where the metaphorical "broken window" is often possession of a small amount of recreational drugs, the crime rate did indeed go down, because an unconscionable proportion of young black men are in jail, where they can't soil the statistics by breaking windows or anything else.

Jim Horn, Associate Professor of Educational Leadership at Cambridge College, Cambridge, MA, describes KIPP's approach:

> (It is) intended to create a culturally-sterilized corps of black order takers and low level corporate drones who never complain and always ask How High? when the boss man says, Jump. If the KIPP neo-eugenic treatment can be perfected by Seligman (psychologist Martin Seligman) and David Levin (co-founder of KIPP), America may finally be on the road to ridding itself of the inferior and depraved cultures that are responsible for poverty and its effects, and we may herald a new day when the unfit accept their own responsibility for their unfitness and, then, work

double time to make up for their own shortcomings that
keep them from entering the gritty corporate bubble where
down always looks up, where everyone keeps on the sunny
side of an increasingly shady Wall Street. [88]

Horn's rhetoric is certainly inflammatory, but his critique
is on point.

With less inflammatory style, but equally alarming detail,
the *San Francisco Chronicle* reported in 2003 [89]:

Students must walk in quiet, single-file lines at all times.
There is a contract for each student – a document signed
by parent, principal and child attesting to their commit-
ment to education. All KIPP kids learn chants and hand
signals that teachers use for everything from teaching
multiplication tables to getting them to recite their college
ambitions.... school hallways are decorated with posters
bearing KIPP slogans such as 'There are No Shortcuts'....
KIPPsters everywhere earn or lose weekly 'paychecks' that
can be spent in the student store. Miscreants are placed
on the bench, must wear signs around their neck that say
'BENCH,' eat at a quiet table and write letters of apology
to each student before explaining to the class how they
will change their behavior.

Quoting Howard Berlak, educator Robert Skeels reports
on the education blog *Schools Matter* that some KIPP schools
actually print "MISCREANT" on the signs to be worn. [90]
Throughout their punishment they are to be shunned. Other
students will be punished if they speak to a miscreant. (The dic-
tionary offers "scoundrel, reprobate and lowlife" as synonyms
for "miscreant").

This is not limited to KIPP schools. A Calhoun faculty member worked for a time at Democracy Prep, another highly celebrated set of New York City charter schools. I earlier in Chapter 2 described a young man, Jamal, who was one object of this abusive policy. This is Democracy Prep's behavior policy at the time my colleague taught there:

AIM:

The goal of the yellow shirt policy is to use the power of social isolation to reform the behavior of children who have been extremely disrespectful, either continuously over a documented period of time or on one notable occasion.

Policy:

Students will be placed in a yellow shirt at the discretion of the Dean of Students after consultation with the Founder and/or Assistant Principal. Students will only be yellow-shirted after they have received an out-of-school suspension.

To earn back their uniform shirt, yellow shirted students will need to:

1. *remain out of detention for 5 consecutive days*

2. *make a public apology in which they are accountable for their mistake (i.e. describe the mistake in detail) and then explain how the mistake caused harm to the team and family. The apology should also include an explanation of how they will change in the future.*

3. *wear a white t-shirt for another 5 school days while remaining out of detention*

After completion of the above steps, the scholar will earn back his uniform shirt.

While wearing the yellow shirt, the scholar will observe the following yellow-shirt protocol:

1. *Not speak to any other scholars – at all – during before-school-time, transitions, in class, at lunch, during advisory, or after school at any time, including bodegas, or public transportation, on the phone, email, IM, etc.*

2. *Sit in the back of the classroom, not near any other scholars.*

3. *Walk at the front of the line, immediately behind the child carrying the clipboard. The yellow-shirted child should be the very last to get in line and when given permission to stand, should calmly take his or her place in line.*

4. *Not speak aloud in class AT ALL. This means:*

    a. *The scholar may not participate in pair-share activities.*

    b. *The scholar <u>may not</u> answer questions aloud in class.*

    c. *The scholar <u>may not</u> ask questions privately to the teacher during work time.*

    d. *The scholar <u>may not</u> sit near enough to any other child so as to be tempted to whisper or speak at all.*

5. *Yellow-shirted scholars will eat standing in the cafeteria, separate from all other children. They will be the last to get their food and will walk up from lunch with the Dean.*

6. *Yellow-shirted scholars will have daily check-ins with the Dean of Students each day until they earn back their regular uniform shirt. The daily check-in will take place during the last 15 minutes of afternoon advisory. It is up to the advisor to decide when to send the yellow-shirted child to see the dean. The child should, under no circumstances, dismiss themselves.*

7. *Any other scholar seen talking to a yellow-shirted child – for any reason – will be given automatic detention. Please make sure to set up your classroom procedures so none of our other scholars are given the opportunity to communicate with the yellow-shirted one.*

8. *Any yellow-shirted child who is seen speaking – for any reason – to another scholar will automatically serve detention that afternoon.*

If a child fails to earn his way into at least a plain white shirt for more than three weeks after he or she is given a yellow shirt, then the Dean of Students will begin to work with the family to seek alternative arrangements for the child.

Now consider this – several presidents, including Barack Obama, have praised Democracy Prep. That our President endorses this treatment of young men and women of color is rather astonishing, but that is the state of educational reform in America. I can't say with certainty that these disciplinary policies are in place at all KIPP or Democracy Prep Schools, and they may have softened their policy language in response to criticism. But the policies and language I've described represent a clear and consistent approach to children and discipline in many urban charter schools – and it is inexcusable.

The contrast with progressive schools could not be more striking. The very progressive Summerhill believes in the essential goodness of children, and offers unfettered freedom as the milieu for their emotional and ethical development. The ultra-conventional charter schools believe that students, almost exclusively poor students of color, must be tightly controlled and civilized. A child does indeed have to be mighty "gritty" to survive what these schools are dishing out.

Anthony S. Bryk and Barbara Schneider provide additional evidence of the critical importance of relationships in school in their 2002 book, *Trust in Schools: A Core Resource.* [91] Among the research findings they summarize are studies that show a profound correlation between levels of student/teacher trust and academic achievement. The schools studied were in poor, Chicago neighborhoods, much like those served by the rapidly proliferating KIPP and other charter schools. It is unlikely that warm, trusting relationships can develop in intimidating no-excuses schools like those I've described, staffed with inexperienced teachers, like Teach for America recruits, who come and go through the turnstiles of the factory model they serve.

I don't dismiss the real issues faced by teachers in urban schools, where students arrive at the doorstep with many, many disadvantages, whereas schools like Summerhill enroll students of relative privilege. But that doesn't justify the disparate treatment. What is being done to black boys and girls in these schools is shameful. I cannot imagine the parents in my school tolerating even one day of this kind of demeaning treatment, which seeks to drive kids into conformity. But it also isn't necessary. These children will respond to love and trust too. Several personal anecdotes reinforce this point.

In 1966 I entered Army basic training in Fort Benning, GA. In this brutal context a few of us were elevated into "leadership" positions each week. I put quotes around "leadership" because we trainees were all Private E-1 in rank, and the leadership roles were just play-acting. I was appointed platoon leader for a week. In this role I had to delegate various menial tasks to members of my platoon – cleaning toilets, sweeping floors, etc.

One of my platoon members was known as Miami Larry. Like about half of my fellow draftees, he was a young black man from a rough part of a rough city. Rumor had it that Larry kept a switchblade under his mattress. He also refused to do much of what he was told to do, a true miscreant by KIPP or U.S. Army standards. However, my standing as a faux leader was going to be judged by my effectiveness in getting all platoon members to do their jobs. It was clear, or so I thought, that no one else was going to do anything if Larry didn't have to do anything. The general basic training ethic instilled by drill sergeants was that we were to manage these things on our own. They didn't want to deal with any problem soldiers unless (their words) "we dragged them to headquarters unconscious." I was not going to, or be able to, render Larry unconscious. It was a dilemma, and the other soldiers were watching with keen interest, as it was chore time and I was on the spot.

After a few minutes of anxiety, I took a risk. Larry was sitting, looking sullen, on his bunk bed. I walked over and sat beside him. He turned slowly and, if such a thing is possible, glowered at me with surprise. I said something like this – "Hi Larry! I'm Steve. I've got a problem. I'm the platoon leader this week and I'm supposed to get everyone working. It seems pretty clear that you don't feel like working, and I understand that. But I'm really in a bind. If you don't do anything, no one else will do anything either – and I'm screwed. I also know that you could kick the crap out of me if you really wanted to, which I hope you don't (nervous chuckle – from me, not Larry, as he was inscrutable and amazed at the same time, if that's possible). So I wonder if you'd do me a big, big favor. Just go over there and pick up a broom. Give the floor a few strokes, walk around a bit. I don't care if anything really gets swept up, but it will sure help me out."

Larry's amazement turned into the slightest curl of a smile at the corner of his mouth. He got up, grabbed a broom and said to the others, "C'mon y'all, get to work." He swept the floor for 30 or 40 seconds, then sat back down on his bunk. But all others did their jobs. I don't mean to romanticize. Larry was discharged some time later under less than honorable conditions. But even in this extreme circumstance, an angry young man responded to my clumsy effort to have a relationship, to be honest, and to treat him with respect. I suspect Larry had very few of these things from the authority figures in his life.

Later, at the end of my military service, I was a First Lieutenant in charge of an administrative unit in Thailand. The unit was a holding company for enlisted soldiers, many like Larry, who were being discharged under less than honorable circumstances. It seems delightfully coincidental that my progressive education instincts were apparently already at work! In defiance of convention (and to the irritation of the Captain to whom I reported) I invited all of these difficult young men to call me "Steve" instead of "Sir." This respectful nod to their humanity made a great difference, and we survived our last months of military service together with good humor and cooperation.

Several years later I began work at a home for emotionally

disturbed children. I dislike the term "emotionally disturbed" because it was invariably the families of these sad kids who were more emotionally disturbed than the kids. It was a residential campus with separate cottages for each 10 to 12 kids. My cottage consisted of boys ranging in age from 12 to18.

My very first shift was from 3-11 p.m. To my surprise and chagrin, the person with whom I was scheduled to work had called in sick. The day shift staffers barely said "hello" and "goodbye" before walking out the door. Some orientation! If you have any awareness of "emotionally disturbed" teenagers, you might imagine my dismay. I didn't know the kids, I didn't know the rules, and skittish teenagers don't respond comfortably to complete strangers.

The boys were nowhere to be seen. For the first few minutes they ignored me entirely. After a while, an occasional face would lean around a doorframe for a quick glimpse before disappearing. Finally, a seemingly well-composed boy stood in full sight for a few seconds. I gestured him over to the chair I'd taken in the cottage living room. I asked his name. "Louis," he replied. "Louis," I said, "I need a favor. Would you please ask all the guys to come down to the living room for a few minutes? I'm new and I'd like to meet everyone." Louis, thank goodness, shrugged, said "ok," and went to collect the crew.

When this odd bunch of wary teens had gathered, I tried my Miami Larry technique. "Hi guys. I'm Steve. I'm new and I don't have any idea what I'm doing. It's my first day. I don't know you. I don't know the rules. I'm alone. So, here's the deal, I'm going to sit here in the living room. Since I don't know what you're supposed to do – or not do – I'll just trust you to do whatever you should. If anyone wants to come and talk with me for a minute, I'd like that. But you don't have to. I only have one request. Please don't run away. If you feel like running away, wait until tomorrow. I'd probably lose my job if someone ran away on my very first day. So, nice to meet you!"

The most remarkable thing happened. The boys drifted off and I began hearing snippets of conversation like, "It's your night for setting the table. C'mon, just do it." Every one of them came by, at least for a minute or two, and talked with me. At dinnertime, they seemed like a finely tuned machine – serving, cleaning up, sweeping the dining room and settling into evening routines. They enforced the "lights out at 10" rule even though I didn't know it existed.

Again, I don't mean to romanticize. I worked there for 3½ years and never had a night quite that easy again! Louis was deeply troubled. Kenny ran away frequently. Steve had a hair trigger temper. Scott was admitted at age 17 after successfully running a small medical practice for a few months before he was caught. There were rare instances when some level of strict control or discipline was necessary – for safety. But the work, even with these challenging boys, was always most successful when they felt trusted and loved. Not when they were made to wear "MISCREANT" signs or be shunned by adults and peers as a consequence for the slightest infraction. It should not be just places like Summerhill where children can be loved and trusted.

I'm acutely aware that these examples might invite criticism that I am comparing students in urban charter schools to emotionally troubled children and soldiers. Quite to the contrary. My intent is to point out that warm, supportive relationships are possible and powerful even in the most difficult circumstances, thereby inviting readers to question why anyone would support "no excuses" discipline with small children who only want to be loved.

In slightly different ways the relationships between students and teachers are central to the progressive philosophies of Rudolph Steiner schools, the schools inspired by the Reggio Emilia Approach, and the hundreds of progressive and democratic schools scattered around the world.

Progressive schools invariably describe themselves as student-centered. In the disparaging caricature of progressive education, which I hope I effectively dismissed earlier, "student-centered" is equated to letting kids do whatever they want, praising kids too much, or spoiling them rotten.

Student-centered actually means something quite different. A progressive school begins by centering the learning process on the actual students in the school, rather than on an external mandate, a common curriculum developed by a publishing company, or by some abstract notion of a theoretical "average" child. Student-centered is both a collective and individual understanding.

The collective understanding is enormously important and is too often ignored. In designing a school's intentions, one must know the children's culture, the experiences and interests they bring to school, and the norms and values shared in their families and communities. As I asserted in my challenge to the Common Core, it is ineffective and culturally insensitive to design learning experiences that have no relevance to students. And yet schools everywhere operate on the assumption that all children have a common collective experience, and we can therefore have one textbook, one set of expectations, and one set of cultural and social assumptions that are valid for every group of students. This concern is at the heart of the work that has been done to identify the way in which many standardized tests, including the SAT's, are deeply biased, advantaging students who come from the majority culture.

The individual idea of "student-centered" has several aspects. As explicated earlier, children develop at different rates, so a good teacher must know where each student is on a developmental continuum. As Gardner and neuroscience have shown, children are intelligent in complex and different ways, and a good teacher must have some understanding of each child's unique abilities.

So, in both the collective and individual realms, no school can be fully effective without taking a student-centered approach. It has nothing to do with spoiling the kids.

Another element of student-centered is the idea of student choice. A fundamental concept of progressive education is the idea of children being agents or architects of their own learning. Philosophically, this has its roots in a naturalistic view of children and in the considerable overlap between progressive education and democratic education. Summerhill and other free, democratic schools are quite clear that students have a fundamental human right to make choices about what they learn. And, particularly at Summerhill, they even have a choice as to whether they will attend classes at all. This idea has long been emotionally and philosophically appealing, but now it appears that it may also have a very powerful neurobiological benefit. It would be reasonable to conclude that student choice is useful if for no other reason than it makes learning more motivating and exciting, thereby stimulating the release of dopamine and enhancing the formation of memories. So why wouldn't we allow students to choose topics, or the approach to learning a topic?

For a kid who loves sports, use baseball statistics to draw her into learning math. I recall a student who was indifferent about some parts of our curriculum and didn't particularly like writing. When given a choice, she researched and wrote a remarkable interdisciplinary essay on French horror films. Another student, in my own class, wrote a brilliant piece about Norwegian heavy punk metal rock (or something like that). Had she been expected to write about Jane Austen, I suspect her work would have been indifferent and hasty. Allowing her to explore within an area of her intense experience and interest led to a wonderful piece that might well have been publishable in a major magazine.

I could give countless examples of how progressive schools use students' own interests to draw them into real intellectual work. But student choice may have an even more powerful biological component than previously recognized. I first learned of this intriguing piece of the stress/learning puzzle in a *Newsweek* article several years ago that, among other things, examined the effects of exercise on stress and stress reduction.

Exercise has long been known to be effective in stress reduction or management. In this study, two stressed rats were yoked together on a pair of exercise wheels. One rat had the ability to initiate exercise, the other had to exercise when and only when the first chose to do so. Rat #1 benefited as predicted – exercise reduced stress and his brain "bloomed with new cells." Rat #2, exercising at precisely the same time and rate, lost brain cells. Researchers concluded that:

He (rat #2) was doing something that should have been

good for his brain, but he lacked one crucial factor: con-
trol. He could not determine his own workout schedule,
so he didn't perceive it as exercise. Instead, he experienced
it as a literal rat race. [92]

This at least hints at the biological benefits of work that is chosen over that which is imposed.

More recent research by Ricardo Mario Arida and others at the Federal University of Sao Paulo in Brazil [93] has affirmed this positive impact of "choice" over "coercion."

Nearly all conventional school practices are designed by adults and then imposed on students – in effect, placing children on exercise wheels over which they have little control. A rat race. These are all reasons to support the very progressive notions of "student-centered" and "student choice."

Chapter Nine

Democracy, Diversity and Empathy

One of the central notions of American progressive education is the role education must play in sustaining our democratic republic. This means, as John Dewey most powerfully described, an inextricable connection between schools and the society in which they exist. While there are many purposes of education, preparation for thoughtful civic engagement is key among them.

One expression of this intent can be realized in either conventional or progressive settings. Knowledge of democratic institutions and principles is important, whether "taught" in a conventional way or "experienced" through progressive pedagogy. This intent is imperfectly addressed in some schools, but increasingly absent in others. In this regard, the charter and voucher movements present significant risk to our democracy, as some pretty weird ideologies and religious fundamentalism are being supported by public funds. And, of course, there are some states (notably Texas), where a particularly conservative, jingoistic version of American history is served up.

Conventional education can teach civics, but again a progressive approach offers a more profound way to sustain a vibrant democracy. In progressive education, children live a democratic experience. In progressive schools, children learn about community, interdependence, empathy, and responsibility.

Diversity

In these times, there is no democratic notion more important than diversity. Race and class have increasingly segregated our nation and its schools at a time when the nation is rapidly becoming more diverse. Conventional public schools are exacerbating these differences. Perhaps counter-intuitively, private schools have become more diverse. And progressive schools are arguably the most actively engaged in the hard work of empathy, justice and understanding. Diversity is hard work – but it can be enchanting too. My very first experience at the Calhoun School is a case in point.

I arrived at Calhoun's Lower School building on the afternoon of my first day of interviews for the Head of School position. I was to meet the director and have a tour. School had just ended and I was a few minutes early. I was directed to a small conference room to wait. In the conference room I encountered two girls seated at the table – one white, one of color– who appeared to be (later confirmed to be) kindergarten age. I sat at the table with them, to their great curiosity and amusement. I introduced myself, asked their names and posed a series of kindergarten-appropriate questions about school, what they were interested in, and so on. I was surprised to find them fully comfortable chatting with a middle-aged stranger. I've come to know with experience that this comfort and confidence is a lovely consequence of a progressive environment where all students are important individuals from the first day in school. These girls had been at Calhoun for 2½ years and just saw me as another peer human, albeit older and bigger.

After a few minutes of banter, the girl of color paused, glanced at her friend, then looked me right in the eyes and said, "We're sisters, you know." For a school that doesn't give many tests, she was offering up a doozy. The impish look on her face was priceless. Just what exactly would the strange, older white man have to say about that?

Without skipping a beat I replied, "Twins?" She and her friend giggled with appreciation. I passed the test. At that moment I knew I'd take the job if offered.

This small story is not just cute. There was a great deal embedded in this short, humorous exchange. She was testing to see if I would shy away from recognizing racial identity. She was offering a preposterous lie to see if she could bait me into saying or thinking, "No you can't be, because you're black and she's white." She wanted to see if I had a sense of humor. How many 5 or 6 year-old children could conjure up such a complex test of identity awareness?

Another test came several years later. A Calhoun Middle School teacher of color approached me to talk about his younger brother. The younger brother, in 8th grade at a New York City public school, was drifting toward trouble, at least in the judgment of his older sibling. The younger brother was bright, but disinterested in school and spending more time on the street. "Might Calhoun find a place for him?" asked our teacher.

It seemed that the younger brother would be unlikely to gain admission to a private school based on the typical criteria. The older brother had gone to a private school by virtue of an organization called Prep for Prep, which places kids of color in private schools and, as the name implies, "preps" them for the experience. Even though Calhoun does not require test scores and assesses a rich variety of qualities, we do select from a large pool of applicants. It's one of the aspects of private school reality that I don't like. This young man might not be among those we would ordinarily admit, but I decided that sibling preference was more than justified. It would cost the school nothing at all to offer a chance. But I had one stipulation. I wanted to meet with him and make sure that he wanted to come to Calhoun. It would not be successful if it was only his older brother's idea and that he would therefore not be invested in making it work. We met.

During a 30-minute conversation, he convinced me that he wanted to give it a try. He was honest about his ambivalence. He didn't see himself as a private school kid. He recognized, as did I, that students of color often have a challenging time in a majority white school. He (and I) knew his friends on the "street" would give him a hard time. But, on balance, he thought it worth a shot. I did too, particularly because he was honest, not trying to "sell" me. But then he threw me for a loop.

"Before you leave, is there anything you'd like to ask me?" I said. "Yes," he replied. "What would you think of me if you saw me on the street?"

He had come to the meeting with saggin' pants, a wide brimmed cap and some heavy silver jewelry. It seemed quite intentional, as he was surely sophisticated enough to know that khakis, blue oxford cloth and polished loafers might be more typically "private school." Not so much at Calhoun, but he probably didn't know that.

I tried not to laugh, but couldn't repress a smile. "Honest answer?" I asked.

"Yes," he responded.

"If I saw you on the street I'd think, 'what a sweet looking kid!'" He looked incredulous.

"But I know why you asked the question. Let's talk about that."

We had a conversation about what he meant. Would the school require him to surrender his identity? How many stereotypes about "young black men" would he encounter? And much more. It was a complex and courageous thing for a 14 year-old to explore. He did indeed attend Calhoun and it was not easy, especially at first. But he was, as I anticipated, a wonderful student. He became a real student leader, a voice for justice and equity, and a warm, funny, delightful human.

Diversity is most frequently thought of in racial terms. A racially integrated school or community is diverse, a mostly white or mostly of color community is not. But for purposes of looking at conventional versus progressive philosophy, the idea of diversity is more complex. A truly diverse school should be reflective of all the important human differences – race, gender, religion (or lack thereof), sexual identity, temperament, intelligence, ethnicity, culture and others. What most distinguishes, or should distinguish, "progressive" from "conventional" in this context is that progressive schools acknowledge and embrace these aspects of a student's being while many conventional schools insist on conformity.

When discussing diversity at Calhoun I emphasize this distinction to help families determine whether we are the school they wish for their children. My experience suggests that diversity in many conventional schools is simply a matter of assembling kids of different races in a culturally homogeneous environment. The implicit, if not explicit, agreement is, "We will invite your child into our school with the expectation that he/she will conform to the norms and values of the school." This expectation may be expressed in uniforms, dress codes, curricula, social conventions, "acceptable" speech, traditions, and other overt and subtle ways. Despite the unspoken or subtle nature of the values, the implicit message is clear. "You're welcome if you conform and assimilate."

At Calhoun and other progressive schools, this idea is turned on its head. Our explicit agreement is, "We will invite your child into our school with the expectation that we will learn from and appreciate her identity, life experience, culture, values and interests. We will try to adjust the school's norms and values to accommodate and embrace hers (and yours)." This has many implications for a school community.

The importance of diversity work has never been greater. In the summer of 2016, racial tension and police violence shattered America's equilibrium. In response to a gratuitous attack in the New York Post on school diversity programs, like those in Calhoun and other progressive schools, I wrote:

White privilege is neither an indictment nor a fantasy. It is simply fact. I and other white folks in America have benefitted from several centuries of advantage. We had the opportunity to chart our own destiny, to accumulate capital, to own property and to live in relative safety while generations of black women, men and children were enslaved, raped, lynched, denied the rights of citizenship, redlined, blackballed, blue-shielded and otherwise denigrated. It's easy to declare that the playing field is level when you built it on a slope and you're standing on the top of the hill.

The assertions about kids "being made to feel awful about their whiteness" are nonsense. My colleagues and I at Calhoun, and our friends at Bank Street and other schools, have done this work for years. It is true that children may initially feel uneasy in these conversations, but it is the uneasiness that unlocks the door to understanding. Acknowledging white privilege is not assigning guilt. Guilt is not useful. White people, including students, work toward equity when they feel empowered, not guilty. Compassion, empathy and understanding are the goals of any good diversity work. It is a liberating experience to understand one's privilege and to embrace the opportunity and accept the responsibility to be part of necessary change.

We are deeply divided in America. Some people believe racism is a thing of the past, that black folks are playing the victim, that affirmative action is reverse racism and that the answer to racial tension is for people of color to shut up and work harder.

Others recognize the corrosive effects of racism and pov-
erty, the ongoing reality of mass incarceration, the barriers
to employment, chronic despair, stop and frisk policies,
racist taunts directed at the President of the United States
and yes, the shameful litany of boys and men of color
shot by police without provocation. My colleagues and I
in progressive, diverse, independent schools hope to raise
a generation of these "others."

Individuation

As described previously, adolescence is a time of "second phase" individuation. It is when the developing young adult is most acutely examining his or her identity and place in the world. Insisting on conformity at this stage inhibits this work. One might argue, "But they can do all of that at home. School is not the place." I would counter that school is absolutely the place, because home is often more restrictive for various reasons. But more to the point, working toward individuation and individual expression is most powerful and important in the peer environment – testing, trying things out, and experimenting. Schools also have, or should have, skilled faculty and staff to guide this crucial stage of adolescent development in a safe environment. Homes or neighborhoods are not always safe or fertile environments for this kind of growth.

Rather than avoiding "a whole lot of trouble," strict codes and enforcement can magnify the alienation that Jacquelynne Eccles described in schools where authoritarian control is the norm. The "trouble" is just driven undercover and can emerge in unhealthy ways. This doesn't mean that kids in progressive schools can do whatever they want (even at Summerhill), but the absence of strict, inflexible rules inspires really important conversations.

I've long held the view that you should not have rules for children unless you can explain the rationale. It is a very good test for the rule setter, since the inability to explain the rule ought to lead to its reconsideration. I had a relatively unimportant experience like that in my first year at Calhoun. I was sitting with a group of upper school kids, mixed grades, and the topic of elevator privileges arose. The existing rule was that seniors could ride the elevator – no other students, unless temporarily or permanently physically limited. To younger students this was a grave injustice. We had a fun conversation about the rule. I suggested that limited elevator capacity and the population in the building seemed to require a rationing policy. We reached consensus on that point. Then we also reached consensus (reluctantly, on the part of juniors) that rationing the resource by seniority was as reasonable as any other system.

Then the seniors in the group challenged me. The existing policy allowed seniors to ride the elevator up, but not down. "What was the rationale for that?" they asked. Well, I thought to myself, if anything it would make more sense for them to walk up and ride down, at least as a health matter. I pondered for a few seconds and couldn't think of any reason to support the "walk down" policy. We changed it instantly.

If you ever long for a really divisive and colorful dinner table conversation among friends and relatives, bring up the topic of dress codes or uniforms in schools! Often dress codes, particularly as applied to girls, deal with sexuality and objectification. If we set "no cleavage," "no bare midriff" and "no short skirt" rules, what is being conveyed? One camp argues that such rules are an authoritarian way to shame girls into thinking their sexuality or their bodies are taboo. Another camp argues that girls should be discouraged from dressing to appeal to their male peers, because such behavior is subordinate and disempowering. I don't write to support one camp or the other. My larger point is that this discussion is much more important than the rule. Testing and questioning these issues is an important learning experience.

There are many reasonable proponents for dress codes or uniforms. The standard arguments are that strict dress expectations reduce the use of clothing to signal wealth or status. Uniforms or standardized clothing requirements are great equalizers. I know. I was in the Army. Many educators and parents also contend that commercialized clothing or sexualized attire detract from a school's educational mission. Having strict standards saves everyone from a whole lot of trouble. A more progressive view, at least mine, is that the "whole lot of trouble" is an important developmental and learning opportunity.

Arbitrary and meaningless rules ought to be challenged and changed. If a rule is "just because," and has no rationale that a teenager can or should be able to understand, then the teenager may feel justified in dismissing the entire architecture of discipline and behavior. For example, the idea that a shirt must have a collar seems a stuffy convention. On the other hand, a ban on commercial messages on clothing has a supportable rationale whether one agrees or not. Something that titillates or intimidates might well be sanctioned while something that innocently expresses identity ought not to be arbitrarily prohibited. Rules about hair length or color, for example, seem intended to repress individuality rather than to maintain a civil, peaceful community.

If we expect students to develop critical capacities and to make ethical and thoughtful decisions, we should give them practice. The most effective way to do this is to include students in the establishment of rules. It may surprise some adults to find that students, when given this trust and responsibility, will often make more draconian rules that the adults would have instituted.

So, the strict structures that characterize many conventional schools shortchange the growth and development of adolescents. But rules, norms, conventions and tradition are even more damaging when considering a diverse group of students. Dress codes and culturally normative rules of conduct may stifle a very significant part of a child's identity and culture. Here is my school's dress code as stated in our handbook:

> *Calhoun does not have a detailed dress code. We expect that all students will dress in a way that is appropriate for a school setting and that their choices respect Calhoun's intent to sustain a community that is inclusive of a diverse range of identities. Students who make inappropriate or insensitive choices will be expected to reconsider. Calhoun's expectations for appropriate dress encompass the understanding that gender expression is not binary, that racial and cultural influences may inform students' choices, and that individual self-expression is a natural and important part of human development.*

With a dress code, the devil is in the details. So we avoid them. The policy has multiple intentions. First, we explicitly reject the notion that appropriate attire is gender specific. Our policy also acknowledges the risk that expectations may be based on subconscious racial, cultural or religious bias. The last phrase in our policy is perhaps the most important. We recognize that adolescent expression and identity are developmentally crucial. Repressing this expression with an arcane and detailed dress code is not wise or productive. It is a mistake to pathologize healthy teen-age experimentation.

Years ago, several Calhoun teachers described a 6th grade boy as "likely transgender." Several years later, in 9th or 10th grade, he returned from summer vacation wearing a pair of sparkling women's shoes. "Nice shoes," I commented when encountering him for the first time in September. He smiled and said, "Yeah, I worked in a really cool shoe store over the summer."

Over the following months he gradually established a female identity. Dresses, skirts and other female attire became the norm. This clothing expression was critically important in this student's developing identity. She became increasingly flamboyant. It was, to say the least, an interesting conversation when she had to be reminded that our limits on cleavage applied to all students who identified as female! I recall, with some institutional pride and affection, encountering this student, in a lovely summer dress, skipping arm-in-arm up the sidewalk with the co-captains of the boys' varsity basketball team. This natural evolution of identity and its expression could not have happened in a place where conformity and compliance are central values.

When a school provides freedom of choice and expression, the most excessive expression usually "burns" itself out, because there is no unreasonable authority to push against. A case in point is another student who came to Calhoun in 9th grade.

The identity she initially cultivated was quintessential Goth.

Black clothes, blue hair, black lipstick, piercings, and a little purple once in a while – you get the picture. Nothing about her daily get-up could be justifiably considered offensive, intimidating or sexualized. As we came to know her we learned that the Goth stereotype was silly. She was delightful, a good student, not particularly rebellious and very responsible. On the first day of 10th grade she showed up with a cute Dorothy Hamill hair cut (am I dating myself?), brown linen slacks and a white blouse with a Peter Pan collar. I asked, "What happened to the costume?" She smiled and said, "Oh, that's too much trouble. I don't have time for that in the morning anymore." End of Goth era. But on her terms.

Empathy and Learning

Empathy is drastically underrated. Often confused with its sibling, "sympathy," empathy is a critical part of learning and scholarship. Empathy does not mean "feeling sorry" for someone. Quite to the contrary, it is the capacity to understand another perspective by considering it through the lens of another person, time or situation rather than through only your own. Empathy often involves struggling to understand a viewpoint for which one may have little sympathy.

Empathy should be a daily tonic in schools. We should lead students to better understand a scientific concept by inviting them to consider the views of intelligent skeptics. They should come to understand international conflict, including terrorism, by developing an understanding of the complex experiences that fuel rage in terrorists – not through a simplistic theological belief in good and evil or through a nationalistic lens. They should learn about important social and historical issues by living for a while on the side of the issue most foreign to their initial point of view. And, of course, our students should learn about the diversity of humankind by listening to and empathizing with one another, not by judging one another from the narrow safety of their own experiences. Empathy is both a quality to be appreciated and a muscle to be exercised.

One of my favorite pieces of Calhoun curriculum over the years was a Middle School social studies project that exemplifies many aspects of progressive education. This 8th grade project was comprised of examining a crucial historic event/ era through the mechanism of role-playing in a mock trial. The topic alternated from year-to-year. One year, the abolitionist John Brown was on trial. Was he a criminal or a hero? The next year, the great industrial barons, Carnegie, Rockefeller, Vanderbilt et al, of America's 20th century were on trial. Were they robber barons who plundered America at the expense of workers, or visionaries who raised our standard of living and produced some of history's greatest advances? The moments I describe are from a "Carnegie/Rockefeller" year.

The exercise required each class to divide into two equal parts. One side argued for "conviction" in the mock trial, the other for "acquittal." The students had no choice of team, so many kids were expected to argue a point that differed from their own initial sentiments. In this case, the 8th graders tended to lean toward conviction at the beginning of the process. The students were expected to do significant research into the era, learning the history, the context, the facts of industrialization, the issues of child labor, and so on. Then, research concluded, the trial began. A jury of adults, including me, listened to the arguments over several days and rendered a verdict. Students assumed the roles of key players in the exercise, including prosecutors, defense attorneys, defendants, key historical figures, workers, and anyone else students felt would provide meaningful testimony. They often went to the trouble to dress in clothes of the period and learned to emulate social behavior or language norms from the period.

In the year I'm recalling, several remarkable moments arose. One young woman, Jessica, took on the role of an adolescent mineworker. She came to the trial in period dress, with a bonnet, smudges of soot on her cheeks and a fistful of facts about the abuses of children, their health problems, their stunted physical and emotional development, and other consequences of their harsh lives. During her testimony, both when examined by the sympathetic prosecutor and cross-examined by the lawyer for the defense, she broke down in tears. This was not acting, although Jessica was a capable young actor. She had developed such powerful empathy for the experiences of child laborers that her emotions were fully authentic. At one point, we (the judges) excused her from the stand so that she might compose herself. I could describe many other similar moments from the prosecutors' case.

The defense did an admirable job of quantifying the advances resulting from the age of industrialization. They were remarkably savvy, gently questioning Jessica and others with sympathy, but accurately eliciting the fact that she and her family were even worse off before she got a job in the mine. "Not that we condone your treatment," one defense lawyer said, "but the facts make it clear that our clients, on balance, made the world a better place, including for you and your family."

Then came closing arguments. The lead defense lawyer, Max, closed with a brilliant, entirely original, and unexpected argument. He opened by expressing enormous sympathy for and understanding of the plight of poor folks, workers and children. And then, with statistics, compelling logic, and accurate historical context, he argued that if not for the industrial barons, the world would have succumbed to the Third Reich. It was, he argued, the production capacity and natural resources developed by the industrialists that allowed civilization to triumph over great evil.

"We are eternally in their debt," he closed. "You must acquit." And we did.

Chapter Ten

What Can Be Done?

The social and constitutional aspects of education and education policy are complex. If government, particularly the federal government, is the primary culprit in furthering the dominant factory system of education, then perhaps we should just get the government "off our backs." Tempting, indeed. But wrong.

There is a role for government in education, as in many realms where the promises of the Declaration of Independence and the Constitution are at stake. That role is to affirm that equal educational opportunity is a universal right which is implicitly enshrined in our founders' intentions and explicitly affirmed in case law. The right to educational equity is codified in many states' constitutions and statutes. Here the government's role is clear and unambiguous – in order to assure equal opportunity under the law, government has a role in the allocation of resources and the enforcement of all constitutional protections against discrimination and suppression of rights.

In recent decades federal policy has done just the opposite. Enforcement of equal opportunity has been lackluster at best. The federal government has largely left educational equity up to the states, which have highly varied capacities to meet the challenge. States have passed the burden of education funding to local communities, primarily in the form of property taxes, thereby exacerbating inequity.

While abrogating its responsibility to ensure educational equity, the federal government has become increasingly dictatorial about educational policy and practice, leveraging its relatively small financial investment into an ideological bludgeon. As briefly touched on in these pages, the federal government is influenced by the deep pockets of wealthy education reformers. All in all, the weight of the federal government has been brought heavily to bear on individual classrooms across America while doing very little to insure equality of opportunity. Most egregiously, governmental bodies, federal, state and local, have been accessory to the crime of privatization, further exacerbating segregation by race and class. So equity remains elusive.

The current direction toward privatization in education is equivalent to outsourcing in the criminal justice system. The Corrections Corporation of America (CCA) is the criminal justice equivalent of the education privatization movement that is currently underway. CCA is a $1.8 billion company that builds and operates prisons and detention facilities on behalf of the Federal Bureau of Prisons, Immigration and Customs Enforcement, the United States Marshals Service, and state and local agencies. All of their incentives are perverse. Maximizing revenue depends on "customers" and "repeat" customers. In the decade ending in 2012 CCA spent nearly $18 million lobbying various government agencies to keep the market robust. [94] In their own SEC filing they wrote:

> *The demand for our facilities and services could be adversely affected by the relaxation of enforcement efforts, leniency in conviction or parole standards and sentencing practices or through the decriminalization of certain activities that are currently proscribed by our criminal laws. For instance, any changes with respect to drugs and controlled substances or illegal immigration could affect the number of persons arrested, convicted, and sentenced, thereby potentially reducing demand for correctional facilities to house them.* [95]

Read that excerpt carefully. CCA sees draconian drug laws and punitive immigration practices as good for business. Their interests are diametrically opposed to social justice. It takes only modest revision of the language of the SEC filing from CCA to imagine it coming from a charter organization:

> *The demand for our facilities and services could be adversely affected by proper funding of district public schools and decriminalization of certain activities that currently land young black fathers in jail, particularly with respect to drugs and controlled substances. Any changes that resulted in substantial job creation, fair wages and rebuilding of neglected urban communities might potentially reduce demand for alternative, impersonal "no excuses" facilities to house poor children.*

Here too, the interests are diametrically opposed to social justice.

To be fair, children in urban charter schools are not prisoners, despite "no-excuses" disciplinary practices that might seem prison-like. Even increasingly profitable charter management organizations are not going to benefit from recidivism. Education reformers do want children to succeed, at least on their own limited terms. But there is common ground with prison privatization along several dimensions. As education becomes privatized, the same perverse incentives arise. Ratcheting up class size and increased use of technology reduce labor costs. Reduced labor costs increase profit. The highly mechanized systems being developed by corporate reform are cost effective, replicable and scalable.

In short, many schools driven by education reform are really an aggressive manifestation of the industrial style of traditional education that has dominated education policy for more than a century. The difference – and it is a critical difference – is that this time it's also profitable. That makes it attractive to education corporations and investors, but also makes it really dangerous.

In the 1960's and 70's, educator and author John Holt faced circumstances like those of today. He believed schools repressed real learning and he eventually gave up on efforts to reform public education. He became the most notable advocate of homeschooling, or "unschooling." [96] I admire Holt, as do many progressive educators, but I don't share his belief that public education is broken beyond repair. Surrendering means giving up the historic power of public education to elevate lives, to bring children together across boundaries of race, class, ethnicity and belief, and to draw each child into a rich, satisfying lifetime of ethical citizenship. Homeschooling divides rather than unites. It discourages diversity of experience and can reinforce the provincial beliefs of a family or community. Home-schooling is also a luxury, untenable for struggling families that depend on school as an extension of support for their children. Abandoning public education, either through privatization or escape, will further divide an already fragile nation.

So what can drive real education reform – the progressive revolution that is so desperately needed? There are encouraging signs.

The current version of traditional education has prevailed because we have allowed it to prevail, but millions of thoughtful educators and parents are fighting back. Resistance to the "testing and accountability" era is growing rapidly. Even the most metrics-obsessed educational policy wonks acknowledge that some of their mandates have backfired. There is significant backlash to stressful time-wasting tests and the preparation they require. Test based, value-added teacher evaluations have been discredited. Teach for America is dwindling. Abusive discipline and expulsion policies in charter schools have been identified and remediation called for. Advocates for Children of New York, a non-profit whose mission is "protecting every child's right to learn," issued a scathing report in early 2015 [97] that explicated the inappropriate and sometimes illegal disciplinary practices of many charter schools. *The New York Times* has published several stories about the abusive practices at Success Academies. [98]

Real reform requires that people who know about children and learning be at the forefront of public education. We need fewer economists and more teachers involved in setting policy and developing practices.

We might start by replacing the prescriptive and political

United States Department of Education with a National Commission on Public Education. The Commission would be comprised of experienced teachers, leading theorists, educational
philosophers, child development experts, and neurobiologists.
They, in turn, would appoint a set of regional accrediting
groups, also comprised of educational experts, not economists
or policy wonks. This is very much analogous to the accrediting
systems in place for higher education that, while not perfect,
are effective and led by educators, not politicians or economists.

The regional accrediting groups might be charged with
ensuring that every child be exposed to the arts, literature,
history, science, mathematics, languages and cultures beyond
our borders, current world events, ethics, empathy, health, and
human sexuality. The specifics in each discipline would be left
to schools and teachers. The "how" should be guided by the rich
body of knowledge about human learning and child development that I have summarized in these pages. The accrediting
groups would be charged with monitoring to ensure that the
declared broad purposes and enlightened pedagogy were in
place. Within that framework, supported by small classes and
professional respect, America's teachers would be liberated to
do what so many of them long to do – teach the actual children
in their care, not the abstraction of children addressed by current educational policy and practice.

The problem of charter schools and so-called school choice
is particularly vexing. The charter horse seems long gone from
the barn, but we might at least try to fence in the pasture.
No for-profit school should receive taxpayer dollars. No religious school should receive public funding. All charter schools
should be subjected to the same requirements for financial
and operational transparency as their regular public school

counterparts. Oversight by an accrediting agency, such as that proposed above, should be required of any school receiving public funding.

The growth of the charter industry has been aided and abetted by legislative bodies, particularly state legislatures, around the country. These legislators serve us, not their donors or the lobbyists who press for charter expansion. Our voices must be heard. There is no doubt that the proliferation of charter schools has eroded funding of the public schools that serve the majority of our children. This will continue only if we allow it to continue. Take a stand. Contact your legislators and tell them that your vote depends on their support of public education. Protest against any expansion of charter schools. Write to the local newspaper.

Some years ago my adult children and I had a spirited debate about change. They argued for small, individual acts of kindness, generosity and wisdom. I argued for political movements, massive protests demanding social and economic justice. I've come to believe it is an unimportant distinction. Change is like a good snowstorm, massive drifts created from elegant snowflakes, each one contributing its small part to creating a new landscape.

More than any other single thing, revolutionary reform must be driven by parents who demand a better, more loving experience for their children. I hope this book will reinforce parents' best instincts and provide them with ammunition to demand more (or less of many things!) from their teachers and schools. It is fitting that a progressive revolution be a grassroots revolution. The money and politics that have a stranglehold on education policy can only be changed when we insist on change.

Bill of Educational Rights

Parents and concerned citizens should demand the following things from every school. Consider it a *Bill of Educational Rights*. Turn this list into a petition and circulate it among all the families in your child's school. Send it to the school board, the principal, local legislators.

The undersigned insist that our school(s) and all teachers:

- *Recognize the broad consensus that early childhood education should be primarily dedicated to free, imaginative play;*

- *Provide arts programming, recognizing that the arts are critical to all learning and to understanding the human experience;*

- *Provide ample physical movement, both in physical education classes and in other ways, recognizing that exercise enhances learning for all children;*

- *Exhibit, in structure and practice, awareness that children develop at different rates and in different ways; that strict age- or grade-level standards and expectations are meaningless and damaging;*

- *Acknowledge the large body of evidence that long hours of homework are unnecessary and detract from children's (and families') quality of life;*

- *Exhibit genuine affection and respect for all children;*

- *Honor a wide range of personalities and temperaments;*

- *Encourage curiosity, risk-taking and creativity;*

- *Cultivate and sustain intrinsic motivation rather than relying on elaborate extrinsic systems of rewards and punishment;*

- *Understand that brain research supports active learning, engaging all the senses;*

- *Understand that children are intelligent in multiple ways and that all these intelligences should be honored and developed;*

- *Listen to each child's voice, give them real experience in democratic processes, and allow them to express their individuality;*

- *Know each child well, appreciate the unique mix of qualities each child brings, and never demean, discourage or humiliate any child.*

The simplest test is this – is your child happy and does he/she look forward to school most days? If not, you and your child have the right – the obligation – to demand change. Children should not be subjected to stressful and punitive schools. As I write, a nationwide "opt-out" movement is gaining momentum. All parents have the right to say "no" to stressful, meaningless tests, to keep their children healthy and happy.

The uniform, factory approach to education has never served all children well. The cost is immense. Children who develop more slowly in early years are dismissed as less capable and may internalize this misjudgment for a lifetime. We neither recognize nor nurture children who are brilliant in ways that don't conform to the IQ-style of education and assessment. As a result their growth may be stunted and their potential to contribute to society is truncated. The extrinsic structures that drive compliance and conformity inhibit intrinsic motivation. One of the greatest satisfactions in life is the endless opportunity to learn and grow. When school is a stressful or unpleasant experience, aversion to continued learning is an inevitable consequence.

We should allow our children to grow naturally, not force them into early, unnatural tedium. We should treasure all children's originality, not press them into intellectual or social conformity. This requires igniting their imaginations, cultivating a love of beauty, and instilling a fascination with the natural world.

We desperately need our children to love the world and its people enough that they will save it.

Our purpose should be to sustain curiosity, strengthening children's intrinsic desire to continue learning for a lifetime. We should affirm each child's intelligence, giving all children the freedom to construct their own lives without judgment.

Pursuing these purposes does not contradict the declared intentions of education reform. Rather, it achieves the purposes of education reform. Tedium, stress and conformity are the enemies of both individual satisfaction and social progress. Imagination and beauty are the things that enliven each individual life and advance civilization.

I began by claiming that we are living in a time of unprecedented existential risk. The risks are amplified by surrendering control of education to those who profit from the compliance and control of conventional education. Can we change the world if our children believe climate change is a hoax or that evolution is just another theory? Will the world be safer if schools teach a whitewashed version of history, declaring America "exceptional" and inculcating blind faith and nationalism? Can we expect future generations to change the world if they are not encouraged to challenge conventional wisdom?

The qualities nurtured through a progressive approach to education are the things that animate meaningful lives and promise the greatest contributions to society.

And, above all – first do no harm.

References

1. Grace Paley, 2001, *Begin Again: Collected Poems, Responsibility*, Farrar, Straus and Giroux

2. John Dewey, 1915, *The School and Society*, The University of Chicago Press, retrieved from: https://archive.org/details/schoolsociety00dewerich

3. A. S. Neill, 1960, *Summerhill School: A Radical Approach to Child Rearing*, Hart Publishing Company

4. Conference Board, Job Satisfaction: 2014 edition, retrieved from: https://www.conference-board.org/topics/publicationdetail.cfm?publicationid=2785

5. Wendy Mogel, Ph.D., 2001, *The Blessing of a Skinned Knee: Using Jewish Teachings to Raise Self-Reliant Children*, Penguin Books

6. Jerome Bruner, 1960, *The Process of Education*, Harvard University Press

7. Howard Gardner, 1973, *The Arts And Human Development: A Psychological Study of the Artistic Process*, Basic Books

8. Howard Gardner, 1983, *Frames of Mind, The Theory of Multiple Intelligences*, Basic Books

9. Howard Gardner, 1993, *Multiple Intelligences: The Theory in Practice*, Basic Books

10. Diane Ravitch, 2013, *Reign of Error: The Hoax of the Privatization Movement and the Danger to America's Public Schools*, Alfred A. Knopf/Random House

11. Yong Zhao, 2014, *Who's Afraid of the Big Bad Dragon: Why China has the*

Best (and Worst) Education System in the World, John Wiley and Sons, Inc.

12. Jonathan Kozol, 2000, *Ordinary Resurrections: Children in the Years of Hope,* Crown Publishers

13. United States Department of Education, 1983, *A Nation at Risk: The Imperative for Educational Reform,* retrieved from: http://www2.ed.gov/pubs/NatAtRisk/index.html

14. Tamim Ansary, March 9, 2007, Education at Risk: Fallout from a Flawed Report, *Edutopia.org,* retrieved from: http://www.edutopia.org/landmark-education-report-nation-riskSandia report, *Perspectives on Education in America: An Annotated Briefing,* C.C. Carlson et al, *Journal of Education Research,* v86 n5 p259-265 May-Jun 1993, available for download from http://www.tandfonline.com/doi/abs/10.1080/00220671.1993.9941211

15. Mercedes K. Schneider, 2014, *Chronicle of Echoes: Who's Who in the Implosion of American Public Education,* Information Age Publishing, Inc.

16. Anthony Cody, 2014, *The Educator and the Oligarch,* Garn Press

17. Denny Taylor, 2014, *Save Our Children, Save Our School, Pearson Broke the Golden Rule,* Garn Press

18. Jordan Weissman, February 20, 2013, The Ph.D. Bust: America's Awful Market for Young Scientists – in 7 Charts, *The Atlantic,* retrieved from: http://www.theatlantic.com/business/archive/2013/02/the-phd-bust-americas-awful-market-for-young-scientists-in-7-charts/273339/

19. December 10, 2014, Room for Debate: Are Charter Schools Cherry Picking Students? *The New York Times,* retrieved from: http://www.nytimes.com/roomfordebate/2014/12/10/are-charter-schools-cherry-picking-students

20. Luis A. Huerta, December 10, 2014, High-Suspension Rates at Charter Schools Don't Help Students, *The New York Times,* retrieved from: http://www.nytimes.com/roomfordebate/2014/12/10/are-charter-schools-cherry-picking-students/charter-schools-do-a-disservice-to-their-students

21. Carol Burris, December 10, 2014, Charter School Cherry-Picking From Admission to Expulsion, *The New York Times,* retrieved from: http://www.nytimes.com/roomfordebate/2014/12/10/are-charter-schools-cherry-picking-students/charter-school-cherry-picking-from-admission-to-expulsion

22. Richard D. Kahlenberg and Halley Potter, December 10, 2014, Don't Misunderstand How Charter Schools Succeed, *The New York Times,* retrieved from: http://www.nytimes.com/roomfordebate/2014/12/10/are-charter-schools-cherry-picking-students/dont-misunderstand-how-charter-schools-succeed

23. Bob Herbert, October 6, 2014, The Plot Against Pubic Education: How

millionaires and billionaires are ruining our schools, *Politico Magazine*, retrieved from: http://www.politico.com/magazine/story/2014/10/the-plot-against-public-education-111630

24. Progressive Education Association, *Eight-Year Study: Purpose, Method, Results*, retrieved from: http://education.stateuniversity.com/pages/1947/Eight-Year-Study.html

25. Denise Clark Pope, 2001, *Doing School: How We Are Creating a Generation of Stressed Out, Materialistic and Miseducated Students*, Yale University Press

26. Celestine Bohlen, December 16, 2014, Students See New Hope in Bias Protests, *The New York Times*, retrieved from: http://www.nytimes.com/2014/12/16/education/students-see-new-hope-in-bias-protests.html

27. Ruthann Richter, October 8, 2015, Among teens, sleep deprivation an epidemic, *Stanford Medicine News Center*, retrieved from: https://med.stanford.edu/news/all-news/2015/10/among-teens-sleep-deprivation-an-epidemic.html

28. Sara Bennett and Nancy Kalish, 2006, *The Case against Homework: How Homework is Hurting Children and What Parents Can Do About It*, Three Rivers Press

29. Alfie Kohn, 2006, *The Homework Myth: Why Our Kids Get Too Much of a Bad Thing*, Da Capo Press

30. Amber Arellano, February 16, 2016, Michigan: The Poster Child for How Not to Do Charter Schools, *Huffington Post*, retrieved from: http://www.huffingtonpost.com/amber-arellano/michigan-the-poster-child_b_9210754.html

31. The Education Trust – Midwest, February, 2016, *Accountability for All: The Broken Promise of Michigan's Charter Schools*, retrieved from https://midwest.edtrust.org/accountability-for-all/

32. Jacoba Urist, April 4, 2014, Is College Really Harder to Get Into Than It Used To Be? *The Atlantic*, retrieved from: http://www.theatlantic.com/education/archive/2014/04/is-college-really-harder-to-get-into-than-it-used-to-be/360114/

33. MetLife Foundation, February, 2013, *The MetLife [2012] Survey of The American Teacher: Challenges for School Leadership*, Report ED 542202 (Figure 3.3, page 45), retrieved from: http://eric.ed.gov/?q=MetLife+Survey+of+Teacher+Satisfaction&id=ED542202 http://files.eric.ed.gov/fulltext/ED542202.pdf

34. Julian Vasquez Heilig and Su Jin Jez, January, 2014, Teach for America, A Return to the Evidence, *National Education Policy Center*, retrieved from:

http://nepc.colorado.edu/files/tfa-return_0.pdf

35. Michael Leachman and Chris Mai, May 20, 2014, Most States Funding Schools Less Than Before the Recession, *Center on Budget and Policy Priorities*, retrieved from: http://www.cbpp.org/research/most-states-funding-schools-less-than-before-the-recession

36. Joshua D. Angrist, Susan M. Dynarski, Parag A. Pathak, Christopher R. Walters, May 2010, Inputs and Impacts in Charter Schools: KIPP Lynn, *American Economic Review*, Vol. 100, No. 2, retrieved from: https://www.aeaweb.org/articles?id=10.1257/aer.100.2.239

37. Atila Abdulkadiroglu, Joshua D. Angrist and Parag A. Pathak, August, 2012, The Elite Illusion: Achievement Effects at Boston and New York Exam Schools, *IZA*, retrieved from: http://economics.mit.edu/files/8054

38. School Vouchers: The Wrong Choice for Public Education, 2012, *Anti-Defamation League*, retrieved from: http://www.adl.org/assets/pdf/civil-rights/religiousfreedom/religfreeres/School-Vouchers-docx.pdf

39. Dr. John B. King, Jr., letter dated August 6, 2014, releasing 50% of the 2014 English Language Arts (ELA) and math questions, retrieved from: https://www.engageny.org/file/103221/download/2014_grades_3-8_ela_and_mathematics_tests_commissioner_letter.pdf New York State Education Department Press Release, August 6, 2014, State Releases 50% of Questions from 2014 Grades 3 - 8 Assessments, retrieved from http://www.nysed.gov/news/2015/state-releases-50-questions-2014-grades-3-8-assessments EngageNY, Annotated 3-8 ELA and Mathematics State Questions (2013 & 2014), retrieved from https://www.engageny.org/resource/new-york-state-common-core-sample-questions https://www.engageny.org/file/118406/download/2014-ela-grade-3-sample-annotated-passages.pdf

40. Steve Nelson, August 13, 2014, Our Students. Their Moment. My A**!, *The Huffington Post*, retrieved from http://www.huffingtonpost.com/steve-nelson/our-students-their-moment-my-a_b_5668310.html

41. Joy Resmovits, November 29, 2012, School Testing in US Costs $1.7 Billion, But That May Not Be Enough: Report, *The Huffington Post*, retrieved from: http://www.huffingtonpost.com/2012/11/29/school-testing_n_2214362.html

42. Paul Lockhart, March, 2008, *A Mathematician's Lament,* Mathematical Association of America online web-zine MAA Online, Devlin's Angle, retrieved from: http://www.maa.org/external_archive/devlin/devlin_03_08.html https://www.maa.org/external_archive/devlin/LockhartsLament.pdf

43. Jane M. Healy, Ph.D., 1990, *Endangered Minds: Why Children Don't Think – and What We Can Do About It*, Touchstone

44. Jane M. Healy, Ph.D., 1998, *Failure to Connect: How Computers Affect Our Children's Minds – and What We Can Do About It,* Touchstone

45. Arlene Karidis, February 17, 2015, Blended Learning (Pt 2): Policy Issues and Best Practices, *The Huffington Post,* retrieved from: http://www.huffingtonpost.com/arlene-karidis/blended-learning-part-2-p_b_6658218.html

46. Matt Richtel, Julie Scelpo, Tara Parker-Pope and Marjorie Connelly, 2010, Your Brain on Computers, *The New York Times,* retrieved from: http://topics.nytimes.com/top/features/timestopics/series/your_brain_on_computers/index.html

47. Susan Pinker, January 30, 2015, Can Students Have Too Much Tech? *The New York Times,* retrieved from: http://www.nytimes.com/2015/01/30/opinion/can-students-have-too-much-tech.html

48. Jade Marcus Jenkins, et al, July 6, 2015, Head Start at ages 3 and 4 versus Head Start followed by state pre-k; Which is more effective? *Education Evaluation and Policy Analysis,* 38(1): 88-112, retrieved from: https://www.ncbi.nlm.nih.gov/pmc/articles/PMC4827921/

49. Kathy Hirsh-Pasek, Roberta Michnick Golinkoff, Laura E. Berk, and Dorothy Singer, 2009, *A Mandate for Playful Learning in Preschool: Presenting the Evidence,* Oxford University Press

50. Kirsten Olson, 2009, *Wounded by School: Recapturing Joy in Learning and Standing Up to Old School Culture,* Teachers' College Press

51. Sebastian P. Suggate, Elizabeth A. Schaughency, Elaine Reese, Children learning to read later catch up to children reading earlier, *Early Childhood Research Quarterly,* Volume 28, Issue 1, 1st Quarter 2013, retrieved from: http://web.uvic.ca/~gtreloar/Articles/Language%20Arts/Children%20learning%20to%20read%20later%20catch%20up%20to%20children%20reading%20earlier.pdf

52. Frank Smith, 2003, *Unspeakable Acts, Unnatural Practices: Flaws and Fallacies in Scientific Reading Instruction,* Heinemann

53. Betty Hart, Ph.D., Todd R. Risley, Ph.D., 1995, *Meaningful Differences in the Everyday Experience of Young American Children,* Paul H. Brookes Publishing Co.

54. Douglas Quenqua, October 16, 2014, Quality of Words, Not Quantity, Is Crucial to Language Skills, Study Finds, *The New York Times,* retrieved from: http://www.nytimes.com/2014/10/17/us/quality-of-words-not-quantity-is-crucial-to-language-skills-study-finds.html

55. L. P. Benezet, November/December, 1935 and January, 1936, *The Teaching of Arithmetic: The Story of an Experiment,* Originally published in *Journal of the National Education Association,* retrieved from: http://www.infer-

ence.phy.cam.ac.uk/sanjoy/benezet/ http://www.inference.phy.cam.ac.uk/sanjoy/benezet/three.pdf

56. Michael Winerip, April 8, 1994, A Disabilities Program That 'Got Out of Hand', *The New York Times*, retrieved from: http://www.nytimes.com/1994/04/08/nyregion/a-disabilities-program-that-got-out-of-hand.html?pagewanted=all

57. Richard A. Friedman, October 31, 2014, A Natural Fix for A.D.H.D, *The New York Times*, retrieved from: http://www.nytimes.com/2014/11/02/opinion/sunday/a-natural-fix-for-adhd.html

58. Sarah Zobel, October 6, 2014, Research Finding: Morning Exercise Beneficial to Students, *University of Vermont Communications*, retrieved from: http://www.uvm.edu/~uvmpr/?Page=news&storyID=19250

59. Ritalin Side Effects and Warnings, Updated December 3, 2015, *drugenquirer*, retrieved from http://ritalinsideeffects.net/

60. Mark R. Lepper, Sheena Sethi, Dania Dialdin, and Michael Drake, 1997, Intrinsic and Extrinsic Motivation: A Developmental Perspective, In *Developmental Psychopathology: Perspectives on Adjustment, Risk, and Disorder*. Ed. Suniya S. Luthar, Jacob A. Burack, Dante Cicchetti, and John R. Weisz. New York: Cambridge University Press

61. Sugata Mitra,TED Radio Hour, April 25, 2013, *How Much Can Children Teach Themselves?*, retrieved from: http://www.npr.org/2013/06/21/179015266/how-much-can-children-teach-themselves

62. 62. Jacquelynne S. Eccles, Allan Wigfield, et al, Negative Effects of Traditional Middle Schools on Students' Motivation, *The Elementary School Journal*, Vol. 93, No. 5, May, 1993, pp. 553-574, retrieved from: https://www.researchgate.net/publication/233896434_Negative_Effects_of_Traditional_Middle_Schools_on_Students'_Motivation

63. Denny Taylor, 1998, *Beginning to Read and the Spin Doctors of Science: The Political Campaign to Change America's Mind About How Children Learn to Read*, National Council of Teachers of English

64. Office of the Comptroller, New York City, 2014, *State of the Arts, A Plan to Boost Arts Education in New York City Schools*, retrieved from: http://comptroller.nyc.gov/wp-content/uploads/documents/State_of_the_Arts.pdf

65. Don Campbell, 1997, *The Mozart Effect: Tapping the Power of Music to Heal the Body, Strengthen the Mind and Unlock the Creative Spirit*, HarperCollins

66. Daniel J. Levitin, 2007, *This Is Your Brain on Music: The Science of a Human Obsession*, Penguin Group

67. Kari Leif Bates, May 25, 2007, The Essential Tones of Music Rooted

in Human Speech, *Duke Today*, retrieved from: https://today.duke.
edu/2007/05/essential-tones-music-rooted-human-speech

68. Nina Kraus and Bharath Chandrasekaran, August, 2010, Music training
     for the development of auditory skills, *Nature Reviews Neuroscience*, 11
     (8), 599-605, retrieved from: http://www.nature.com/nrn/journal/v11/
     n8/abs/nrn2882.html

69. Diego Minciacchi, November 2003 (online version January 24, 2006),
     Brain Sciences versus Music, Annals of the New York Academy of Sciences,
     999: 215-217 retrieved from: http://onlinelibrary.wiley.com/doi/10.1111/
     nyas.2003.999.issue-1/issuetoc

70. Gottfried Schlaug, Andrea Norton, Katie Overy and Ellen Winner, 2005,
     Effects of Music Training on the Child's Brain and Cognitive Develop-
     ment, *Annals of the New York Academy of Sciences*, 1060: 219-230 (2005)
     retrieved from: http://www.musicianbrain.com/papers/Schlaug_Music_
     Child_Brain_NYAS2005.pdf

71. Eric Jensen, 2001, *Arts with the Brain in Mind*, Association for Supervision
     and Curriculum Development

72. Dee Dickinson, 1997, Learning Through the Arts, *New Horizons for
     Learning*, Johns Hopkins University, retrieved from: http://education.
     jhu.edu/PD/newhorizons/strategies/topics/Arts%20in%20Education/
     dickinson_lrnarts.htm

73. Mona Brookes, 1997, Teaching Basics Through the Arts, *New Horizons
     for Learning*, Johns Hopkins University, retrieved from: http://education.
     jhu.edu/PD/newhorizons/strategies/topics/Arts%20in%20Education/
     brookes.htm

74. Clancy Blair, February 2002, School Readiness: Integrating Cognition and
     Emotion in a Neurobiological Conceptualization of Children's Functioning
     at School Entry, *American Psychologist*, Vol. 57, No. 2, 111-127, retrieved
     from: https://steinhardt.nyu.edu/scmsAdmin/uploads/006/743/Blair%20
     -%20AmPsych.pdf

75. Sondra H. Birch and Gary W. Ladd, 1997, The Teacher-Child Relationship
     and Children's Early School Adjustment, *Journal of School Psychology*, Vol.
     35, No. 1, pp. 61-79, retrieved from: https://www.gse.harvard.edu/sites/
     default/files/uk/Teacher-Child-Relationship.pdf

76. Jacquelynne Eccles, 1999, The Development of Children Ages 6-14, *The
     Future of Children*, Vol. 9, No, 2, Fall 1999, retrieved from: http://www.
     futureofchildren.org/publications/docs/09_02_02.pdf

77. Scott E. Page, 2007, *The Difference: How the Power of Diversity Creates
     Better Groups, Firms, Schools, and Societies*, Princeton University Press

78. Martin Nystrand, Lawrence L. Wu, Adam Gamoran, Susie Zeiser and Daniel Long, 2001 (online version 2003), Questions in Time: Investigating the Structure and Dynamics of Unfolding Classroom Discourse, *The National Research Center on English Learning & Achievement*, The University at Albany State University of New York, retrieved from: http://www.albany.edu/cela/reports/nystrand/nystrandquestions14005.pdf

79. Robin Wood-Moen, September 27, 2015, Dopamine and Stress Response, *Livestrong.com* http://www.livestrong.com/article/366013-dopamine-and-stress-response/

80. Richard J. Herrnstein and Charles Murray, 1994, *The Bell Curve, Intelligence and Class Structure in American Life,* Simon & Schuster

81. 81. Daniel Goleman, April 10, 1988, An Emerging Theory on Blacks' I.Q. Scores, *The New York Times,* retrieved from: http://www.nytimes.com/1988/04/10/education/an-emerging-theory-on-blacks-iq-scores.html?pagewanted=all

82. 82. David Brooks, December 11, 2014, In Praise of Small Miracles, *The New York Times*, retrieved from: http://www.nytimes.com/2014/12/12/opinion/david-brooks-in-praise-of-small-miracles.html

83. Daphna Shohamy and R. Alison Adcock, October 2010, *Dopamine and Adaptive Memory*, Trends in Cognitive Sciences, Vol. 14, No. 10, retrieved from: http://shohamylab.psych.columbia.edu/content/papers/Shohamy_Dopamine%20and%20adaptive%20memory.pdf

84. Paul Tough, 2012, *How Children Succeed: Grit, Curiosity, and the Hidden Power of Character*, Houghton Mifflin Harcourt Publishing Company

85. Paul Tough, 2016, *Helping Children Succeed: What Works and Why*, Houghton Mifflin Harcourt Publishing Company

86. Angela Duckworth, April 2013, Grit: The power of passion and perseverance, *TED Talks Education*, retrieved from: https://www.ted.com/talks/angela_lee_duckworth_grit_the_power_of_passion_and_perseverance?language=en

87. Howard Gardner, 2013, podcast Beyond Wit and Grit, *The Good Project*, Harvard University, retrieved from: http://www.thegoodproject.org/news-overview/videos/

88. Jim Horn, October 7, 2012, Paul Tough, KIPP, and the "Science" of Cultural Sterilization, *Common Dreams*, retrieved from: http://www.common-dreams.org/views/2012/10/07/paul-tough-kipp-and-science-cultural-sterilizatiion

89. Meredith May, December 29, 2003, *A program trying to turn at-risk youth into scholars*, SFGATE, a website of the *San Francisco Chronicle*, retrieved

from: http://www.sfgate.com/education/article/A-program-trying-to-turn-at-risk-youth-into-2524479.php

90. Robert D. Skeels, February 17, 2009, KIPP Reprise from 2006: Why is Everyone Poor and Smiling? *Schools Matter*, retrieved from: http://www.schoolsmatter.info/2009/02/kipp-reprise-from-2006-why-is-everyone.html

91. Anthony S. Bryk and Barbara Schneider, 2002, *Trust in Schools: A Core Resource for Improvement*, Russell Sage Foundation

92. Mary Carmichael, February 13, 2009, Health: Why Stress May be Good for You, *Newsweek*, retrieved from: *http://www.newsweek.com/health-why-stress-may-be-good-you-82765*

93. Ricardo Mario Arida, Carla Alessandra Scorza, Alexandre Valotta da Silva, Fulvio Alexandre Scorza, Esper Abrão Cavalheiro, Differential effects of spontaneous versus forced exercise in rats on the staining of parvalbumin-positive neurons in the hippocampal formation, *Neuroscience Letters*, Volume 364, Issue 3, 8 July 2004, Pages 135-138, retrieved from: http://www.sciencedirect.com/science/article/pii/S0304394004004677

94. Center for Responsive Politics, retrieved from https://www.opensecrets.org/lobby/clientsum.php?id=D000021940&year=2012

95. Securities and Exchange Commission, 2015, Corrections Corp of America, Form 10-K, retrieved from: http://services.corporate-ir.net/SEC.Enhanced/SecCapsule.aspx?c=117983&fid=9949581

96. John Holt and Pat Farenga, 2003, *Teach Your Own, The John Holt Book of Home Schooling*, Da Capo Press

97. Advocates for Children of New York, February 2015, *Civil Rights Suspended: An Analysis of New York City Charter School Discipline Policies*, retrieved from: http://www.advocatesforchildren.org/node/634 http://www.advocatesforchildren.org/sites/default/files/library/civil_rights_suspended.pdf?pt=1

98. Kate Taylor, February 12, 2016, At Success Academy School, a Stumble in Math and a Teacher's Anger on Video, *The New York Times*, retrieved from: http://www.nytimes.com/2016/02/13/nyregion/success-academy-teacher-rips-up-student-paper.html

About Steve Nelson

Steve Nelson has been Head of School at the Calhoun School, on Manhattan's Upper Westside, since 1998. Calhoun is one of America's most notable progressive schools and serves 750 students, from pre-Kindergarten through 12th grade. Calhoun is particularly well regarded for its commitment to diversity and social justice.

Since 1997 Steve has been a columnist for the Valley News, the daily newspaper in the mid-VT/NH area on both sides of the Connecticut River. He has been a regular contributor to The Huffington Post since 2010, writing about education and politics. Before assuming his current position, he worked as an administrator at Vermont Law School and Landmark College. He is an avid violinist and also served for six years as President of a performing arts school in the Midwest.

Steve has competed in many marathons, triathlons, bicycle races and XC ski races, with steadily decreasing success. He now primarily races the grim reaper.

He is married to Wendy Nelson, has two children, Jennifer and Christopher, and three perfect grandchildren – Quinn, Maddie and Jack.